Gert by Sea

Copyright © Will Sergeant (AKA 'Dr Gertrude Glossip'), 2023
Published by the Buon-Cattivi Press, 2023
Adelaide, South Australia
All rights reserved.
ISBN (PAPERBACK): 978-1-922314-09-3
ISBN (EBOOK): 978-1-922314-10-9

This is a work of creative non-fiction. It contains true historic events but some creative adjustments have been made to protect identifying information, and to represent Dr Gertrude Glossip's colourful character, nature and tone.

Editing by Cameron Rutherford

Book design and cover art by Andrew Crooks

Gert by Sea

Companion book to *Queen of the Walk:
Gertrude's Guide to Gay Adelaide History*

Dr Gertrude Glossip

Buon-Cattivi Press
Adelaide, Australia

Contents

Dedication	7
Acknowledgements	9
Glossary of Key Terms	10
Maps	12
Hello and Welcome	15

Hello Sailor: Queering the Port — 21

Dock One	24
SS Gertrude	25
Missions to Seamen	26
Cruise Ships	27
Maritime Museum	30
Show Boats and Gawler Gert	32
The Australian Merchant Navy	34
The Royal Australian Navy – The 'Real' Navy	35
Vitalstatistix, Waterside Workers, and Bert Edwards	38
Life Blood Centre: Donate, but not if you are…	40
'Passing' and 'St Paul's-on-Piles'	42
Women's Health Centres	44
The Freemasons, AFLW, UCA and Climax!	47

The Gay Bay: Nautical but Nice — 51

Moseley Square	54
Colley Reserve: The Great Drag Race	55
St Peter's and the Anglican Church of Australia	57
Sussex Street… without Zest	59

Contents

Trams, Pride Parades, St Andrews and UCA	61
Art Deco, The Olives, Our Lady of Victories, and MacDonnell Lodge	63
ECH, Charles Jury, College Street, and St John's Row	65
Encounters, Parties, Mansions and Childhood Memories	68
Water Sports	71
Stop the Waves! Climax!	74
Coastal Rainbow Tales	77
Coastal Cruising	80
Semaphore and Seaside Feast	81
Tennyson (Estcourt) Beach	83
Going Down in the South	85
Flying the Rainbow Flag	87
Farewell, Until the Next Walk	91

Dedication

To the memory of the late Ian Purcell AM (1946 to 2016), my much-admired comrade and collaborator, whose inspiration created Gertrude Glossip thirty years ago.

Acknowledgements

There are numerous people and organisations to thank for *Gert by Sea*, my companion volume to *Queen of the Walk*. My publisher Dr Alex Dunkin for again encouraging the project and supporting me through the writing process. Ursula Menz and event managers for Lifesaving World Championship Adelaide 2018 for requesting and sponsoring the first Bay walk. Britt Burton and the History Trust of South Australia for requesting and sponsoring the second Bay Walk.

Courtney Barry, Assistant Curator Exhibitions and History, City of Holdfast Bay, for requesting and sponsoring the third Bay Walk. Cindy Crook, Local History Officer, City of Port Adelaide Enfield Libraries, for requesting and sponsoring the second Port walk. My late, great collaborator Ian Purcell AM who inspired, researched, and wrote much of the first Port walk.

Helen Bock for her marvellous 'Lesbian Semaphore' perspectives. Peter Burke for information and insights regarding the Anglican Church of Australia and our Rainbow community. Paul Marsh for information and insights regarding the Uniting Church of Australia and our rainbow community. I thank Dr Nikki Sullivan for her marvellous Q Role at 'In conversation' events celebrating my books. David and Cameron for their Zest story. Thanks to Paul Paech for the water sports photograph and Kenton Miller for the original Gertrude maps and cartoons.

Numerous gay comrades for their gay seaside stories and perspectives. Feast Festival and South Australia's History Festival for providing the platform for the walks. Feast programs for invaluable seaside material.

And finally, and perhaps most importantly, my Gertrude Groupies, old and new, who have faithfully followed me on these walks.

Glossary of Key Terms

Beat: An Australian term referring to a public space where homosexual men knew they could meet, socialise, and possibly (or hopefully) have sexual encounters.

Camp: A term used prior to gay, particularly amongst homosexual men, to describe themselves and each other, and tying into the theatrical and flamboyant stereotype of a homosexual man.

Expelaloo: A modern, excremental automated toilet that replaced older, functional public lavatories. Gertrude calls these 'expelaloos' because an automated voice informs that doors will automatically open after a short period of time. And they don't have discreet entries as old-fashioned lavatories often did, but open directly onto public thoroughfares so that one can literally be 'caught with one's pants down' if one lingers too long!

Feast Festival: Adelaide's LGBTIQA+ Queer Arts and Cultural Festival held annually since 1997.

Gay: A term used to describe gay men (initially for both men and women), arriving in the 1970s with Gay Liberation. Replaced the term camp.

Homosexual: Same-sex attracted person, historically most commonly used for and amongst same-sex attracted men.

Lesbian: A term reclaimed by radical lesbians in the 1970s and 1980s to differentiate themselves from the term 'gay'. Gay then became the term used by homosexual men; thus the L and G in modern acronym LGBTIQA+

LGBTIQA+: Inclusive acronym for Lesbian, Gay, Bisexual, Transgender, Intersex, Queer, Questioning, Asexual, and allies.

Out: A queer person who is open and public about their individual LGBTIQA+ identity.

Glossary of Key Terms

Outing: The act of openly and publicly declaring one's LGBTIQA+ status. This can be an individual's choice. It can also be the act performed by others on persons who are discreet and private about their LGBTIQA+ identity.

Queer: A formerly derogatory term for same-sex attracted people that has since been reclaimed as an affirmative, inclusive term.

Rainbow: Umbrella term and internationally recognised symbol for the queer community.

Rainbow History Lovers: Gertrude sees this as the most encompassing term to describe the various members of the rainbow community and allies; always said in an inclusive and affirming manner.

Port Adelaide Map

B14	1. Dock One
D12	2. Maritime Museum
C9	3. Queens Wharf
C9	4. Lighthouse
D10	5. Port Adelaide Enfield Town Hall
F10	6. Port Adelaide Visitor Information Centre
F4	7. Waterside Workers Federation (Vitalstatistix)
H6	8. St Paul's Anglican Church
K8	9. Port Adelaide Public Library
J12	10. Masonic Temple

Glenelg Map

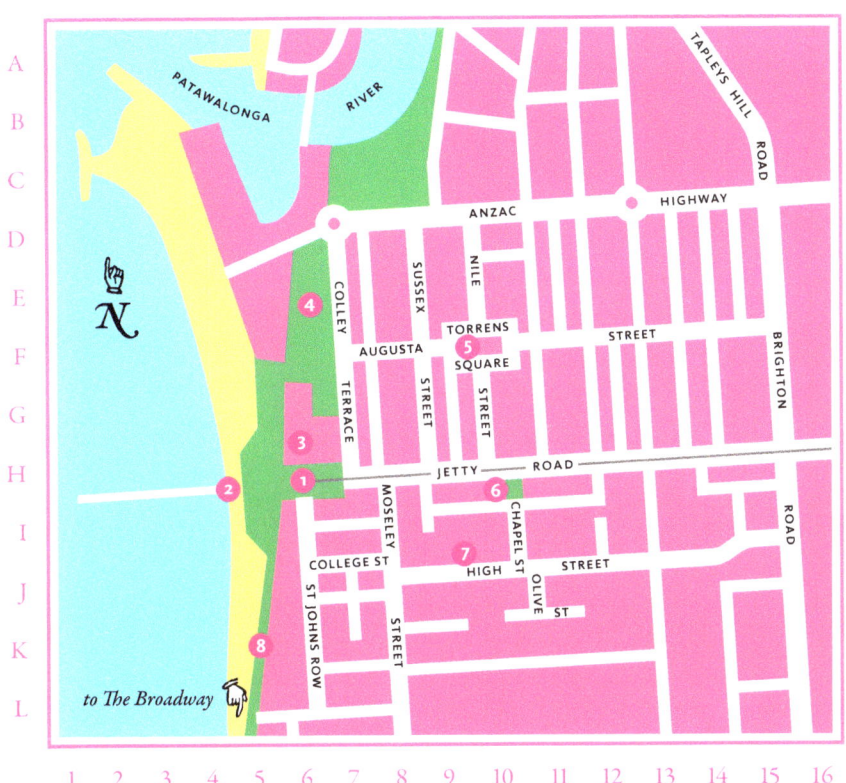

H6	1. Moseley Square	H10	6. St Andrew's by the Sea Uniting Church
H4	2. Glenelg Jetty		
G6	3. Bay Discovery Centre (Former Town Hall)	I9	7. Our Lady of Victories Catholic Church
E6	4. Colley Reserve	K5	8. South Esplande
F10	5. St Peter's Anglican Church		

Gertrude inspects water activities by the jetty.

Hello and Welcome

Naa marni, Rainbow History Lovers. That's 'Hello, how are you?' in the Kaurna language. The Kaurna people are the traditional owners of the land on which our stories take place and on which this book has been produced.

For those who do not know me, let me introduce myself. I am Dr Gertrude Glossip PhD (Formal Drapery) Curtain University, the alter ego of gay activist Will Sergeant OAM. As befits my title my mottos are: decorate while you educate, paint the lily, and add another hue unto the Rainbow. My particular area of interest, and expertise, is Adelaide Rainbow History as manifested in my Rainbow History Walks and my first tome *Queen of the Walk: Gertrude's Guide to Gay Adelaide History*. I was created in 1993 for the Uranian Society, Adelaide's cultural forum for gay men, to lead a history walk. Thus, I celebrate my thirtieth, pearl anniversary, this year. I shall truly be a Pearly Queen! So, it is fitting to celebrate my pearl anniversary by publishing my seaside history walks in book form.

It is lovely to have you all along on my seaside adventure stories, titled so obviously, and appropriately, *Gert by Sea*. Of course, I am going to be devastated if, and perhaps when, the immortal line 'our home is girt by sea' is removed from our national anthem! Like my good self, I think there's something rather quaint and old-fashioned about the term 'girt'!

Now, those who have read my first tome will know it focuses on Adelaide CBD and North Adelaide, as have most of my Feast Festival History Walks. I have conducted history walks at every Feast since its inauguration as the Adelaide Lesbian & Gay Cultural Festival in 1997. As am I, Feast is a jewel in our Rainbow communities' crown.

For Feast 2005, our dear friend and collaborator the late Ian Purcell AM, together with my manager Will, decided I should conduct a 'Port Walk'. We were delighted to discover the oral histories of John Lee (1944 to 1991) contained material about gay adventures and encounters in Port Adelaide. John was a leader in the early Gay Liberation movement in Sydney, Melbourne, and Adelaide. I pay tribute to him in *Queen of the Walk*. In 1979 and 1980 John conducted a series of interviews with forty gay men whose memories dated back to 1910. As with all oral histories the accuracy of information is reliant on the storytellers' recall and perception of events.

As had become our Feast History Walk practice, we conducted a season of two walks which we titled 'Hello Sailor! Or Queering the Port'. It was our ninth Feast season. We had attracted a loyal following by then. The journey down to 'the Port' was seemingly no deterrent. I'm not sure, therefore, why we had not repeated this successful walk.

The second series of my seaside Rainbow History Walks was conducted at 'the Bay', yes Glenelg, that enduringly popular seaside suburb, the birthplace of the British colony of South Australia. Historically, these two areas are quite contrasting: working-class, steamy, seamy Port Adelaide with its varied maritime history, and toney suburban Glenelg with prosperous denizens and holidaymakers. However, as you will discover, 'the Port' is undergoing gentrification with stylish waterfront residential developments.

How did I come to choose 'the Bay' as a suitable location for Rainbow History Walks? Were there gay tales in the John Lee interviews? Be patient, Rainbow History Lovers. All will be revealed… in due course.

Now, we Adelaideans love it when we host international events and are on the world stage! This was indeed so when Adelaide hosted 'The Lifesaving World Championship Adelaide 2018' with over five thousand athletes from forty-four countries competing. Will was delighted when approached by Events Managers for this stellar championship to conduct a Rainbow History Walk focusing on Glenelg, the location of many of the championship's events. Fortuitously, the championships were to be held in November which coincided very nicely with Feast. Thus, we set about ascertaining whether there was sufficient Glenelg Rainbow history. Thankfully there was! Stories from John Lee's oral histories, personal stories of Will's, 1970s Women's and Gay Liberation events and even a Premier Don Dunstan tale!

November 2018 was also the first anniversary of the successful marriage equality postal survey and there were three rather grand churches on our route. This afforded a marvellous opportunity to assess these denominations' response to our Rainbow Family and same-sex marriage. So, it was green light – go!

The Feast program entry read:

> **NAUTICAL BUT NICE**
> *Gertrude goes Bayside*
> PRESENTED BY: LIFESAVING WORLD CHAMPIONSHIP ADELAIDE 2018.
> A Feast Festival first: Gertrude goes bayside. Join Queen of the Walk in this seaside historical extravaganza. From the birthplace of South Australia to present day Glenelg, Gertrude has gay tales to tell. Celebrate Lifesaving World Championships! Bottoms up! buoy ahoy! Be there or be square.

There was mainstream press coverage too with Adelaide's *The Advertiser* publishing a gorgeous photograph of me on Glenelg beach, flanked by four very youthful and toned surf lifesavers, two men and two women, with the caption, 'Gert by Sea: Feast Gets Nautical'.

We are thrilled the World Championship presented the walk, because we believe the embrace of sporting bodies, elite and community, of our Rainbow Family is particularly important. The walk was scheduled for the Sunday of the championship, when a range of community events were being held, so my walk was to be an integral part of the community program. The walk attracted my rusted-on Gertrude Groupies, local folk and those attending World Championship events. This diverse audience was heartening. Staff from the History Trust of South Australia were also present. Such was the appeal of the walk, they implored me to consider repeating the walk for their next festival. And of course, I obliged. I do like to be accommodating. Thus, my second session of walks at Glenelg took place during South Australia's History Festival in May 2019. There was a slight rebadging. The program note read:

> **Gert by Sea: The Bay Gay History Walk**
> Holdfast. Buoy ahoy! Back by popular demand. Following her Feast triumph for Lifesaving World Championship Adelaide 2018 Dr Gertrude Glossip returns to Glenelg.

Again, there was mainstream media coverage in *The Advertiser* with the caption, 'Dragging up bygone stories' accompanied by a very gala photograph of me beside the Town Hall building.

Oh, Rainbow History Lovers, should one overstate one's case or should one strive for modesty and understatement? Be that as it may, the walk was again well-attended and received, with a diverse audience. It is always pleasing when local folk add anecdotes. At our Broadway beat stop a local recounted with humour how, as a young man, he was cautioned about using this facility because of the gay activity there.

But wait, there's even more! In 2022 the lovely Courtney Barry, Assistant Curator of Exhibitions and History for the City of Holdfast Bay (which includes Glenelg), asked me to 'do it all again' for South Australia's History Festival 2022. It is encouraging when local government embraces our Rainbow Family. And the City of Holdfast Bay is one which flies the Rainbow Flag from municipal buildings during Feast. I again answered in the affirmative and conducted my third successful season. And the program note? Well, only minor rebadging was required:

> GERT BY SEA: THE GAY BAY HISTORY WALK RETURNS.

Now, accepting this gig was not without conflict. You see, having just accepted the Glenelg gig, the lovely Cindy Crook, Local History Officer of the City of Port Adelaide Enfield (PAE), approached Will requesting a Port Adelaide Rainbow History Walk for the History Festival. Such were our History Festival commitments, including emceeing the opening event and conducting Dr Duncan memorial walks, we felt we could not accommodate another walk. Thus, we offered Cindy 'the Port Walk' for Feast 2022. And the rest... is history as they say. We were particularly keen to honour our dear friend and collaborator Ian Purcell AM (1946 to 2016). Ian had written the Feast program note for the 2005 walks and had also chosen the image of me. We used both again. And so, the program note read:

> GERTRUDE GLOSSIP AND THE CITY OF PAE LIBRARIES
> HELLO SAILOR: QUEERING THE PORT!
> FEAST RAINBOW HISTORY WALK SEASON 26
> In memory of Ian Purcell AM.
> Ahoy, ye landlubbers! All aboard The Gertrude for a nautical but nice 'cruise' of the queer history of Port Adelaide. Our experienced captain, Queen of the Walk, Dr Gertrude Glossip, will safely navigate the 'dangerous swamps', wharves, pubs and back alleys of The Port to give you magical maritime moments to remember!

Dear Ian! Did have a way with words did he not, Rainbow History Lovers?

Hello and Welcome

And so, I, with sixty walkers, took to the streets of 'the Port'. A good number were local people. It was wonderful to have two of Ian's sisters attending. You see, Ian and his siblings had grown up in nearby Semaphore. There was another group of Semaphore locals too. It was led by a friend who'd been so inspired by the 2005 walk she'd organised a 'staff development walk' for her colleagues at the Port Adelaide Community Health Centre following that walk. Oh, Rainbow History Lovers, you can just see how I love to make connections, be it people, places or streetscapes. This is particularly important for you, my readers, who are on this virtual tour. I want to 'paint the picture' so you feel you are really there.

Let's now go down to Port Adelaide to begin our first walk 'Hello Sailor: Queering the Port'. As we do so I ask readers to be mindful that *Gert by Sea* is designed to be a companion tome to *Queen of the Walk: Gertrude's Guide to Gay Adelaide History*. However, there may be some information, facts, characters and situations that appear in both tomes. For 'Gertrude Virgins' this will be exciting new information. For my rusted-on 'Gertrude Groupies' it will surely be a delightful refresher!

Hello Sailor: Queering the Port

Gertrude mid-presentation during her 2005 Port Adelaide Rainbow History Walk. At the time styled 'Gay History Walk'.

Hello Sailor: Queering the Port

Welcome to our maritime adventure 'Hello Sailor: Queering the Port'. As you will learn, some stories and details come from the original 2005 walks and updates have been incorporated from the 2022 walk. Before we set off, a couple wee trigger warnings. There are some 'colourful tales' with language which was appropriate to the tale and the teller. I believe it is particularly important we hear these tales as spoken at the time, in the voice, and in the words of those who have provided us with their oral histories. Dear Ian, Will and I love context and streetscapes so you will be treated to these too! So, let's proceed on our tour.

Dock One
Renewed Port

Here we are on the waterfront at historic Port Adelaide, now known as 'Dock One'. As we gaze up the Port Adelaide River we do get a sense of an industrial, working port. I am going to regale you with three seaside tales here. But first, just look at those smart ultra-modern terrace rows, known as Dock One Stage 1, which now line the dock. What change has been wrought in recent times? A far cry from the 'rough and tumble' of a busy working port of bygone times.

Let's take a good hard look at our current location. If you hold up a map of the area's coastline, what do you see? Yes, that's right: a long strip of land with a knob on the top. What does it remind you of? It looks very phallic to me!

Now, this phallic landmass, named Mudlangga or Lefevre Peninsula, is bound by the ocean on its western flank and Yerta Bulti or the Port Adelaide River and Estuary region on the east. The British colony of South Australia was founded in 1836 when Governor Hindmarsh and the first colonists arrived down the coast at Holdfast Bay. The new settlement needed a port and town planner Colonel William Light settled on the sight right down at the head of this river because it was deemed the most accessible spot for the new inland township of Adelaide. However, it was not very accessible for ships that had to venture all the way down the river. It quickly became known as Port Misery because it was surrounded by swamps and mangroves and only small vessels could reach it. There was no wharf of course and passengers and goods had to be landed from flat-bottomed boats. Early colonist Alexander Tolmer, who had the 'pleasure' of arriving here considered its name 'well deserved', described the river as a creek and 'the landing of passengers, who were carried ashore on the sailors' backs, and their luggage thrown promiscuously on the muddy beach, and unless promptly removed, frequently damaged by the rising tide.'

Well, well, Rainbow History Lovers, what a way to arrive in the new colony! I think I might have rather enjoyed being carried ashore on the back of a handsome sailor, but as for my precious luggage being 'thrown promiscuously' on the muddy beach with the threat of a rising tide damaging my gorgeous frocks? Definitely not! You will be pleased to hear Port

Misery is definitely 'off our beaten track' so we shall not be venturing there.

Not surprisingly, under the second governor, George Gawler, work began on a wharf about halfway along the river course at the present McLaren Parade location, in the vicinity where we are now standing. A new road, one and a quarter miles (about two kilometres) along New Port Road, was built across the swamp, the whole project costing thirty thousand pounds! Oh, Rainbow History Lovers, just imagine what that would be in today's dollars! I'm sure it was a hefty financial impost for the embryonic colony. However, it was reportedly a proud day for the colony in 1840 when the road and wharf were opened. Five thousand folk, a third of the colonist population, gathered at 'the Port'. It was described as the 'greatest gala day' in the colony's brief history. Unfortunately, a fearful gale blew up and folk had to beat a speedy retreat to the city. It was described as 'an inglorious ending to an auspicious celebration'. Mercifully, we've been blessed with clement weather on each of my Port Walks! So, Rainbow History Lovers, let's move on to our second story at this site.

SS Gertrude
Port River

Rainbow History Lovers, as we continue to gaze up the Port River, I want to tell you a tale about a namesake of mine, the *SS Gertrude*. Did you know such a vessel existed? How very appropriate and fortunate for this little tome it did. Dear Ian was very excited when he discovered this and could not resist including a story about 'The Gertrude' for our walk. As I have commented in the introduction Ian could not resist referencing The Gertrude in the Feast Program:

> Ahoy, ye landlubbers! All aboard The Gertrude for a nautical but nice 'cruise' of the queer history of Port Adelaide. Our very experienced captain, Dr Gertrude Glossip, will safely navigate the dangerous swamps, wharves, pubs and back alleys of The Port.

Dear Ian was being creative. Of course, we did not set foot on or in the water and indeed remained landlubbers. I was certainly not going to allow my stylish, and expensive, footwear to be water damaged.

You see during the Great Depression, Port Adelaide had the worst unemployment rate in Australia. The Port Adelaide Central Mission became very concerned and in the early 1930s its director had the bright idea to purchase a fishing vessel so some of the unemployed fishermen would have work again and the poor people of 'the Port' would have a cheap and nutritious food supply. So, he talked philanthropists Tom Barr Smith and Sir Langdon Bonython into funding the scheme. Both these men were notable South Australian benefactors, the grand Bonython Hall and Barr Smith Library at the University of Adelaide, are but two examples. In 1931 the metal-hulled fishing steamer the *SS Gertrude* arrived from Geelong, and for several years the scheme was indeed a great success. But by the spring of 1934 she was laid up because fishing was not proving economical. The last we hear of her was in January 1935 when she was running free trips for the children of unemployed families. What a worthy vessel! Bring back *SS Gertrude* I say. Oh, Rainbow History Lovers, can't you just picture the scene of me relaunching the *SS Gertrude* with a fine bottle of South Australian bubbles? What a wonderful tourist adornment she would be, don't you think? I could conduct historic river cruises!

Missions to Seamen
Todd Street

Before we move off, Rainbow History Lovers, I want you to cast your eyes inland down Todd Street. We could not have a queer port walk without mentioning the Missions – yes, missions, not emissions – to Seamen. That's about as good as my phallic land mass don't you think?

From 1908 to 1980 the institution located over there at 7 Todd Street was run by the Church of England. There's a Blue Heritage Plaque in acknowledgement. The Mission's symbol was The Flying Angel. Its role was to provide a sanctuary for seamen after long and arduous voyages. There was a chapel with services that were apparently not well attended. There was a games room, a library, a reading and writing room, and accommodation. There were film nights, socials, and dances. The local young women, Portonians, acted as hostesses. No alcohol was allowed. Given seafarers' reputation for hard living, I suspect the whole concept was to try to offer seafarers 'a healthy alternative', as we would say today.

It was the favourite charity of some prominent Adelaideans too. Three generations of women from the famous merchant family, the Haywards (owners of John Martins Department Store), were leading lights in the 'Harbour Lights Guild', indefatigable fundraisers, even holding Gift Teas in the ballroom of the 'top end of town' South Australian Hotel. It is said they were 'quite undeterred by its [the Mission's] social and economic inferiority'.

Another Port Angel was Miss Emilie Miethke. She was the eldest of eight sisters, none of whom married, and four of whom were famous teachers. Oh, Rainbow History Lovers, do you think there might possibly have been a queer tale or two there?

And then there is Frederick Lakeman, wealthy partner in another famous Rundle Street department store, James Marshall & Co., which later became The Myer Emporium. He died a bachelor at eighty-five. His obituary described him as 'one of Adelaide's leading businessmen and philanthropists' whose 'special hobby was Missions to Seamen'. In 1928, he was responsible for establishing and funding the mission branch, The Lakeman Institute, at Outer Harbor. It was a fine building with an imposing, two-storey facade featuring twin-turreted towers. Sadly, it was destroyed by fire in 1992. I'm fascinated by a wealthy old bachelor with a passion for Missions to Seamen! Oh, Rainbow History Lovers, there goes my Rainbow gaze again! With the decline in seafaring trade these organisations have long since ceased operating.

Now, let's proceed on a delightful waterfront ambulation to our next stop and story. Oh, feel the caress of the gentle river breeze!

Cruise Ships
Timpson Street Maritime Memorial

Rainbow History Lovers, here we are at the head of Timpson Street. Oh, look! A maritime memorial – a ship's helm and two mounted plaques. What do they memorialise? The Australian Merchant Navy service in WWI and WWII. More on the Merchant Navy soon (page 34). I do like to keep you in anticipation! It's cruise ships I am going to discuss here. I want you to gaze up the Port River. As I have described, Outer Harbor is situated at the tip of the phallic landmass. As the nineteenth century progressed and ships became larger, it became obvious a deeper port outside the river would be needed. Let's face it, the Port Adelaide River is really very modest in scale! Indeed, ships' captains were sometimes reluctant to make the journey down the river, even to this halfway mark, and either bypassed South Australia altogether or anchored off the coastal suburbs of Semaphore, Largs Bay, or Glenelg and sent launches ashore.

Thus, it was decided to excavate a channel from suburban Largs Bay to the tip of Mudlangga or Lefevre Peninsula and so create a deep seaport. Work began in 1903 and was completed in 1908.

This coincided with the emergence of steamships and ocean liners which were not only transporting migrants to 'the New World' but also travellers making sea voyages for pleasure and recreation. These larger vessels required large crews of stewards to service passengers. There is a theory employers had the policy to employ single men 'of a certain disposition' as a protection for female travellers. Ah, the golden, glamorous age of sea travel, especially if you were travelling first-class and dining at the captain's table, between the 1880s and 1960s. And then mass air travel stole their trade. In the twenty-first century we have seen a resurgence of huge ocean liners as cruising has proved to be so popular.

Now, in terms of passenger travel, there were large ocean liners doing long-haul overseas routes landing at Outer Harbor, and then the coastal trade – smaller vessels travelling around the coast of Australia – using this Inner Harbour as their port. The Adelaide Steamship Company, established in 1875, was prominent in this coastal trade.

The wonderful book *Hello Sailor! The Hidden History of Gay Life at Sea* by Paul Baker and Jo Stanley is awash with gay seafaring tales. It details a very gay life amongst the crew of these commercial ships: shared cabins, dress-ups, and crew messes, which were known as gay bars. It is estimated ninety percent of the stewards on P&O liners were gay men. Of *The Canberra*'s maiden voyage in 1960 a crew member quipped, 'I could honestly say... there was a thousand crew... five hundred gays on that ship... it was heaven'.

And this was at a time when homosexual activity would have been illegal in many ports, and probably not very welcoming to gay seafarers. But on board, as a crew member commented, 'I don't know about it being illegal. It was obligatory dear!'

It is interesting to speculate to what extent there would have been interaction with crew from large ocean liners and local gay men when these ships were in port. Can you imagine what it would have been like, Rainbow History Lovers, when the word got around *The Canberra* was berthed at Outer Harbor with five hundred gay crew? Traffic jam all the way down Port Road! It gives a whole new meaning to naviGAYtion, doesn't it?

Certainly, in the oral histories told to John Lee, there are tales of local gay men frequenting 'the Port' to encounter seafarers, particularly with the crew from cargo vessels and the coastal passenger trade which docked at this Inner Harbour. Apparently, Wednesday was the best day for interstate trade, and provided good opportunities right through into the 1960s. As one interviewee stated, 'Very rarely would you be able to say that there was a steward that was straight. There were of course, but they were exceptions.'

There could be parties onboard too. Another of John's interviewees recounted one such party on *the Avalon*. Apparently, there was a group of local gay men. One of them did a drag performance dressed in a leopard skin frock with matching bra and panties. He did a strip number for the sailors. He then described 'getting off' with the crew. On this occasion the police arrived. At the time he was naked in the captain's cabin – with the captain. One friend jumped overboard and spent some hours in the freezing water before he was game to emerge. The storyteller recounts scampering with his clothes 'to the top of the ship' where he got dressed. Well, well, that is quite a tale! They do say danger can be an aphrodisiac, don't they? We must remember, Rainbow History Lovers, that in South Australia until 1975 all male-to-male sexual activity was criminalised so there was real danger if police 'caught you in the act'.

Let's proceed a little further along the waterfront. Here we are at the corner of Lipson Street and McLaren Parade. We are about to head inland. Before doing so I want you to observe our location. What a charming streetscape with fine facades. On our left a charming two-storey building with its intricate ironwork balcony established in 1850 and, on our right, the striking Art Deco entrance of the Harbors Board building and next-door Country Arts SA, which was the headquarters of the former Adelaide Steamship Company. I'm fascinated by architectural contrasts. Within just a stone's throw of each other, there are the frills of the nineteenth century and here the bold, almost austere geometric lines of the twentieth century on our right.

Maritime Museum
Lipson Street

Rainbow History Lovers, here we are at the South Australian Maritime Museum in the lovely historic precinct of Lipson Street. It is named after an early Harbourmaster, Captain Thomas Lipson, and boasts some fine nineteenth-century architecture. A number of its buildings are heritage listed. The museum building was constructed in 1857 for Elder & Co. and is a fine example of Victorian warehouse construction. The museum was opened in 1986 as part of Jubilee 150, the sesquicentenary of the British colonisation of South Australia. It is now an award-winning museum which is operated by the History Trust of South Australia. Will and I have had considerable connection with the trust and its annual History Festival in which we regularly feature.

Of course, I do think there are several important aspects lacking. I don't believe there is any celebration of the steamier, seamier side of seafaring life. I like the idea of a permanent exhibition in the cellar, as if one were down in the dark hold of a nineteenth-century seafaring vessel! It would have indeed included gay aspects. Now, that would have atmosphere. If the museum was concerned about frightening school children or sensitive adults there could be 'Adults Only' signage with a trigger warning. But that might be even more enticing, don't you think?

There are gay men I am told for whom the sailor or seafarer provides many an erotic fantasy, being referred to by such names as 'seafood platter' or 'sea cake' – white, tight pants with flare and uniforms with lots of gold and braid. I believe it was Winston Churchill who acknowledged the navy ran on 'rum, bum and baccy'. And as we have learnt and will learn again today, there was much sex, and much of it same-sex, to be had both offshore and on. They say the 'short-arm parade' at the ship's doctors after a port stop is a time-honoured naval tradition. Oh, Rainbow History Lovers, are you experiencing 'visuals'? I am!

Let me finish this little segment with a quote from *Hello Sailor! The Hidden History of Gay Life at Sea*:

> Some men simply used the dark unused spaces of the ship. Dave remembers one of the main trysting sites was 'up on the forecastle',

behind the winches. You'd be joking about how the grease off the cable came in handy. We used to call it Forecastle Head Follies. If we had passengers, then it was out of bounds during the days as they could look over and see. But in the dead of night, there'd be no cargo lights on, so it was all pretty dark up there. Any activity going on behind the great winches might be spotted from the bridge, which was higher than where the passengers would be. If the activities got a bit heavy, with bums bouncing around, then officers might get a bit panicky and think, 'God, passengers might see that going on.' They'd flick the cargo lights on a couple of times and that would put the fear of holy Moses into people and they'd scarper. It would calm everything down until next time.

Oh, Rainbow History Lovers, that leaves me a little breathless! I think I'm in need of some bracing waterfront air, aren't you? Let's head back towards the waterfront along Divett Street. Be mindful of the charming facades, some with Blue Heritage Plaques.

Here we are at the Commercial Road corner. Look at this striking marbled entrance. So Art Deco! Will tells me how John Lee introduced him to Art Deco. Such appreciation of this art form was 'compulsory' in their youthful Gay Liberation group of the 1970s. This building is now the offices of Mark Butler MP, Federal Labor Member for Hindmarsh and currently Minister for Health and Aged Care. And behold, a Rainbow motif on the front door with the caption 'WELCOME HERE'. Most encouraging! Across the road at two rather grand nineteenth-century buildings. Look at that turret. I do love a turret! And adjacent there's a charming stone and redbrick building which now houses the Port Adelaide Information Centre. At our last stop I shall tell you about an important exhibition held there during Feast 2022 (page 49). One should always have more to look forward to!

Rainbow History Lovers, let's head up to the waterfront, appropriately named Queen's Wharf, at the top of Commercial Road.

Show Boats and Gawler Gert
Queen's Wharf

We stand before this charming 1869 lighthouse, which was first erected at the entrance to the Port Adelaide River. It later did time on South Neptune Island and was relocated here for Jubilee 150 in 1986. Behold, to our left the massive 'galvo shed', which stretches way down the wharf, emblazoned 'Fishermen's Wharf Markets'. In recent decades it's housed myriad stallholders selling a vast array of merchandise. These markets were highlighted in Feast's 'Seaside Feast' of 1999 and 2000, describing them as 'heaven'! This once-thriving market hub closed in September 2022, just before our Feast History Walk. How sad! Wouldn't that have been an audience, Rainbow History Lovers? Throngs of shoppers gazing upon us or perhaps even joining us? I wonder what its next incarnation will be; upmarket townhouses similar to Dock One perhaps? Seemingly there have been numerous proposals including a car park and a retirement home. What do you think might be appropriate for this historic site?

It is in this location Kaurna elder Hyamiitpinna lived with his family group. He was reportedly the first Kaurna man encountered by the newly arrived English colonists and known by them as King Rodney. There's an important interpretive sign to Hyamiitpinna and the local Indigenous people at the entrance to the Information Centre just down the road.

As we stand before this iconic lighthouse with river breezes gently caressing us, I want to recount two stories here from the oral histories collected by John Lee. In former times, before queer life in Adelaide was so open and abundant, it was often hard to find a place for a 'camp do', an interviewee told John. This was at a time before the word 'gay' became widely used. Homosexual men in particular, generally used the expression 'camp'. Heterosexual folk were then referred to as 'squares' – just to differentiate. So, camp folk had to be creative about finding suitable venues. In the 1960s one of the doyens of the drag camp scene, Beulah Harris, found what she described as a 'showboat'.

There are two accounts of the camp parties which occurred on this showboat. Is it possible there were two sets of these showboat parties? As with all oral histories, some details differ and reflect the storytellers' own memories and recall. One account describes the showboat as 'only a barge with a dance floor', another as 'an old showboat – like a Manly Ferry'. One said everyone was in drag, the other said, 'I wouldn't say that it was all drag, people used to go in drag, but it was a fancy dress ball'. One recounts about four such parties, another that 'there were lots of them each year'. But what can be said for certain, was on at least four occasions, a showboat was hired for these camp parties at which about a hundred camp men would attend, many in drag and fancy dress. They would drive down to 'the Port' in their drag and board the showboat for an evening of fun as it cruised up and down the Port River. The parties were described as 'crowded' and 'fabulous', like a 'floating cabaret' with a band. It seems it was very participative too, with various folk 'doing numbers'. One interviewee said he would do 'Marbella Marguerita', and another recalled 'Angel' arriving dressed as a nun and doing the twist.

Finally, there's a rather amusing story about a namesake of mine. She was known as 'Gawler Gert' and described rather cruelly as 'the ugliest person ever seen'. At one party Gertrude got rather drunk so they stuck her down a hole at the end of the barge with the driver and his fox terrier. Periodically her lipstick-smudged face would appear at the hole exclaiming, 'How are all my beautifuls?' to which she would be greeted with, 'Get back down the hole you bitch!' Well, well, no 'mincing of words' there!

Rainbow History Lovers, there's a modern update to 'cruising' the Port River. In the Feast's Seaside Feasts, Feasters were urged to 'take a river cruise of 2 hours or more' with the enticement of possible dolphin sightings. Seaside Feast 2000 climaxed with a twilight cruise aboard the *MV Port Princess* with entertainment by 'sassy songstress Libby O'Donovan'. And in 2013, as part of Movable Feast-Metro, there was 'The Dolphin Drag & Disco Cruise' departing from this very spot. The program enthused:

> 'Move over Saturday Night Fever – Thank God it's Friday'. The 'captain of the ship' was none other than celebrated Adelaide drag king Ben Dover. Dress Code: drag, nautical, cross dressing encouraged.

Well, well, rather a case of drag queens in the 1960s and drag kings in the 2010s. What fun!

Now, Rainbow History Lovers, enough of this frivolity, partying and drag. Let's continue our promenade along the waterfront and hear about The Australian Merchant Navy.

The Australian Merchant Navy
Birkenhead Bridge

Rainbow History Lovers, here we are at Nelson Street with the Birkenhead Bridge on our right. Let's talk about the Merchant Navy. We've observed the tributes to this navy at our stop back at Timpson Street (pages 27-29). These are the ships involved in commerce, as opposed to passenger ships or the 'real' navy of our defence force. Cargo ships might carry a few passengers, but nothing on the scale of ships devoted to passenger trade. It was a very male environment, not many stewards, very much a working atmosphere, compared with the holiday atmosphere on a passenger ship. So, it was a very homophile atmosphere, of men who liked the company of men. Mostly there would be no women present at all. It was a very discreet, 'uncamp' world compared with the fun, campy atmosphere of the large passenger vessels. The analogy has been made 'between a guesthouse and a Hilton hotel'. It sounds decidedly austere and 'unfun' to me. Give me camp and fun any day!

Now, the cargo ships would berth all along what was North Parade, where we now stand, in a great unbroken line. Of course, this grand promenade was broken in two when the Birkenhead Bridge was built in 1940. Right through until the late 1960s North Parade provided many opportunities for Adelaide camp men to have encounters with seafarers. The Parade would be lined with ships. It was the practice to drive up and down this strip. Seamen would be at work on the ships or just hanging over the sides. There appears to have been a number of pickup techniques. One was to stop and get chatting with the seamen. Another was to frequent the toilet blocks which dotted the parade. One would go in and out several times and loiter about to make it very obvious what one was about.

An interviewee of John Lee recounts:

> Yes, I picked up a number of people that way. I had a fine guy that I picked up there so long ago and he was so beautiful, and I am sure he was Greek or Italian, and he was just a doll, and we had the wildest sex. We parked down at Port Adelaide somewhere… we arranged by sign language that we would meet the following day, by the clock on the car… I was so scared to meet him the next

day and I was too frightened to turn up. I know that he had to leave that day to go on the boat and I had already pinched one guy off the boat and he had jumped ship.

Another explained how one had to be very obvious so he would wear pedal pushers, colour his hair and behave very flamboyantly. 'If you looked like a regular guy, no one wanted you'.

There were stories of going on board. And it wasn't all camp fun. Boarding a vessel could be dangerous. One interviewee explained how they would go onboard as a group and keep each other in sight. 'It was scary onboard,' he said. He recounted the tale of a young man who said 'no' and was treated rather badly. 'They shoved a broom up his arse and threw him off the boat.' This is a rather frightening graphic detail, is it not, Rainbow History Lovers? It was obviously not all 'fun and games'!

Before we move on, I want you to cast your eye over to the British Hotel. We can't have a Rainbow History Walk without at least one pub reference, can we? It is a very old pub, dating back to 1847. After the camp pub scene emerged in Adelaide from WWII onwards, certain pubs, although not strictly camp, were known as 'fringe pubs'. As an interviewee told John, 'Well, you just go in and see a guy on his own and start talking to him… it might take a couple of hours to chat somebody up.' The British was one such pub. It was reputed to be 'good on Saturdays'. Might this have been a popular 'day off' for seamen with plenty of 'seafood platter' on offer, do you think?

The Royal Australian Navy — The 'Real' Navy

Rainbow History Lovers, let's continue our waterfront promenade by crossing Nelson Street and progressing westward. This is our Royal Navy stop. We've chosen this site to recall South Australia's only naval vessel, *HMCS Protector*. Towards the end of the nineteenth century the colony realised its lack of naval protection, especially after the sighting of a Russian naval vessel in its waters. Thus, *The Protector* was commissioned in 1884. It was described as 'the most formidable ship of her size afloat'. Apparently, the only time she ever fired her guns was for the royal salute on South Australia's Proclamation Day on December 28th each year. Across the water is the site of the former *HMAS Encounter* naval yard, which closed in 1994. As I write, it is now 'under redevelopment' with work in progress to create an expansive, upmarket residential precinct. Ah, the changing face of Port Adelaide!

Lieutenant Commander Edward 'Ted' Nichols (1922 to 2017), who had seen active service during WWII, pursued a professional career in the navy after the war and was posted here in 1953 to help prepare for the 1954 royal visit. He retired in 1979. Ted was a gay man. He lived in a commodious house in North Adelaide and won renown in camp circles as the leader of an 'upmarket camp set'. I believe he was humorously styled 'The Rear Admiral' as an acknowledgement of both his personal and professional life. According to the John Lee oral histories he hosted quite outrageous camp parties at his home, one of which is recounted in *Queen of the Walk*.

I've already referred to the Winston Churchill witticism about the navy being run on 'rum, bum and baccy'. My Rainbow gaze suggests that perhaps there was a naval tradition of 'turning a blind eye'. Perhaps officers were too busy 'navel gazing'? My dear late friend Ian Purcell did some research in this regard. In three hundred years of British naval history there appears to be only one documented case of execution for buggery – four sailors from *HMS Africaine* in 1816. In the Seven Years War (1756 to 1763) there were only eleven court martials for sodomy and seven charges of indecency from a navy of eighty thousand sailors (seventy-five percent of whom would have been single).

More recently, in his memoir *Rum, Bum and Concertina* jazz singer George Melly describes the relatively relaxed attitude he found as a seaman in His Majesty's Service after WWII:

> It was accepted for instance, on my mess deck, that on Saturday anyone who fancied some mutual masturbation would crush down in the coat locker room… as relaxed and tolerant an atmosphere as any I've ever encountered.

Peter Nation, the well-known Adelaide antique dealer who was gaoled for alleged indecent assault in 1954, apparently had quite a penchant for sailors. He recounted in his interviews with John Lee various experiences with US marines on leave in Adelaide during WWII. He describes them as very friendly types who would just come up to you in a pub and start talking. He recounted one marine coming up and asking, 'Do you know where we can find some fairies?' On another occasion a US marine visited his antique shop and was 'As brazen as can be. Next thing he said you know, "Put your hand on this". And I said, "For heaven's sake", because at that stage I wasn't terribly into it at all. Well, he was very amusing'.

On the Feast 2005 walk we celebrated several anniversaries. One was the twenty-first anniversary of 'women at sea' – that's right, women in a combat role in the Royal Australian Navy (WRANS). Of course, WRANS have been around much longer than that. Historian Ruth Ford has written about sexuality in the Australian women's services during WWII. She interviewed many women as part of her research. Their stories indicate lesbian relationships were formed within the women's services and authorities were aware of possible lesbianism and sometimes took disciplinary action. For example, one young woman was called before an officer after having a bath with another woman and questioned. On being asked if she were a lesbian, she replied, 'Oh no, I'm a Presbyterian'. She had never heard the word 'lesbian' before and didn't know what it meant.

Betty, who was in the WRANS, recalled two women who were discharged after being caught kissing in the boiler room. Paradoxically, the concern about lesbianism and actions taken by the women's services over suspected lesbian behaviour also contributed to the development of a lesbian identity for women with same-sex desires. They became aware there were others like themselves, and there was language available to define and label themselves.

In 1992, the Keating Labor Government lifted the ban on homosexuals in the Australian Defence Force (ADF). Conveniently for our 2005 Feast walks, in October 2005, the RSL approved a decision to allow homosexual partners of defence servicemen and women access to the same benefits as heterosexual partners: in housing, moving, travel and leave allowances, as well as other benefits such as education assistance. However, the changes did not necessarily allow compensation and superannuation benefits to flow to homosexual partners. In 2009, the Rudd Labor Government introduced equal entitlements to military retirement pensions and superannuation for domestic partners of LGBTIQA+ personnel. Since 2010, transgender personnel may serve openly and may undergo medical and social transition with ADF support while continuing their military service. Cate McGregor's story, which I have covered in some detail in *Queen of the Walk*, is a high-profile example of an officer transitioning.

Rainbow History Lovers, hasn't it been grand to promenade along the waterfront with vistas stretching way up the river? We are now going to head inland again.

Vitalstatistix, Waterside Workers and Bert Edwards
Nile Street

Rainbow History Lovers, here we are in Nile Street at the Waterside Workers Federation Hall. It's a rather imposing facade, freshly painted and emblazoned 'WMA 1926 Waterside Workers Federation,' and a little less prominently 'VITALSTATISTIX THEATRE COMPANY EST 1984'. Indeed, it has been the home of the women's theatre group Vitalstatistix since 1984. 'Vitals', as it's affectionately known, was founded by three new Adelaideans – Margie Fischer, Roxxy Bent and Ollie Black. Margie Fischer AM has made an amazing contribution to Adelaide's Rainbow community, recognised by her Order of Australia honour. She was a founding co-artistic director of our fabulous Feast Festival in 1997. Indeed, she approached Ian, Will, and my good self to stage a Gay History Walk for that first Feast, a tradition Will and I have continued every year since. On our 2022 Feast History Walk, we honoured Feast's Silver Jubilee and Margie's extraordinary contributions.

So, let's explore some of the extraordinary contributions Vitals has made to women's and queer theatre over almost forty years. It was the first full-time women's theatre company in Australia. The company produced new works by South Australian women writers from women's perspectives for a popular audience. And Ollie is also popularly credited as a 'founding member of Lesbian Semaphore' (more about Lesbian Semaphore later in this tome, pages 81-83).

From 1984 to 1996 almost all the company's productions included lesbian characters. Some, such as *The Apron Fashion Parade*, and *The Gay Divorcee* were exclusively lesbian.

Over the years, Vitals has employed hundreds of women as writers, designers, and actors. It has nurtured new works and established a tradition of holding lesbian play readings and the occasional full-scale production. I adore the title of their first Feast offering 'Dyke is not a Dam' which explored 'Dyke style' and posed tantalising questions such as 'Can a Fem fuck a Fem?' Well, well, Rainbow History Lovers, that is food for thought, is it not? Which leads very nicely to the following year's offering 'Fish… a gourmet night for girls'. 'A salubrious salon… girls talking fishy, licking fishy fingers and sipping sumptuous wine'. Oh, doesn't that sound divinely decadent!

Vitals has attracted a loyal general audience and has toured extensively to country centres and other Australian capital cities. It has run three major indigenous music festivals and a number of workshops. The second Artistic Director, Catherine Fitzgerald, continued the tradition of lesbian input. Later, Catherine was artistic director of Feast for the 2013 and 2014 seasons. Another creative leader at Vitals, Helen Sheldon, was head-hunted I believe by Margie Fischer to assume the General Manager role for Feast in 2017. From 2019, CEO & General Manager, Helen continued in her leadership role for six sessions. She was the inspiration and a driving force behind the creation of Adelaide Festival's 2022 stunning oratorio *Watershed: The Death of Dr Duncan*, a world premiere of course! So, you see there's been quite a connection between Vitals and Feast.

An important incident in Adelaide workers' history began in the front of the building on the 9th of January 1931. You see, during the Great Depression roughly one in two working men at 'the Port' were unemployed. The impact of such numbers on family earnings can barely be imagined. Thus, we should not be surprised that frustration and hardship boiled over when the government omitted beef from the ration issue. A group of young men who had congregated on North Parade stopped here to invite the leaders of the Waterside Workers' Federation and the Seamen's Union to join them in their protest march to the city. They marched to the singing of 'The Red Flag' and were joined by others along the route. At Southwark they joined forces with another thousand unemployed people and all together they marched to the Treasury Building on Victoria Square to demand an audience with Labor Premier Lionel Hill.

While waiting for a response, the demonstration turned violent. Bricks were thrown and a police officer was struck with an iron bar as the crowd surged forward. *The Advertiser* reported the police, assisted by 'mounted men', made a concerted charge, 'Within a very short while a furious struggle was in progress and blood was flowing on both sides'. The premier defended the police action and blamed Communist agitators. 'They did not want a deputation,' he said. 'They wanted a riot.'

You will be interested to note Premier Hill lost the next election in 1933 and so began Labor's thirty-two years in opposition.

There is a rather nice gay twist to this stormy tale though. It is reported as the protestors marched past the Newmarket Hotel on the corner of North and West Terraces, every man took off his hat and put it on his rear end, a kind of blokey salute to Labor MP Bert Edwards, proprietor of the Newmarket and a great supporter of workers and their rights, who was on trial for sodomy. I have a very soft spot for Bert, whose extraordinary life is covered in some detail in *Queen of the Walk*. It is a MUST read!

Life Blood Centre: Donate, but not if you are...
St Vincent Street

Rainbow History Lovers, let's proceed down Torrens Place to grand St Vincent Street. Oh, look! What do we have on the corner? Australian Red Cross Life Blood Centre with a billboard emblazoned 'Why wait to donate? Come in and give life today'. I don't believe the centre was in situ when I conducted my walk in 2005 but I certainly made a point of including it in my recent 2022 walk.

Now, we all know Australia has an excellent record of voluntary blood donation. Upon the advent of the HIV and AIDS epidemic, sexually active gay men were discriminated against because of the fear of transmission of HIV through donations. For years gay men were actually banned from donating blood. Subsequently, declarations of celibacy for the preceding twelve months were required. Seemingly, it was irrelevant that gay men could demonstrate HIV-negative status, or that they were in a monogamous relationship, or that they declared they always practised safer sex. And this was in an era where blood was checked for the presence of HIV regardless. This banning of donations also applied to others from the most affected communities, including sex workers, and IV drug users. The 'celibacy waiting period', as I call it, was reduced to three months in 2021. However, the following restrictions still apply to this day:

If you answer yes to any of the following questions you will have to wait three months:
- Had oral sex with another man, even 'safer sex' using a condom (if you are a man)
- Had sex (with or without a condom) with a male who you think may have had oral or anal sex (with or without a condom) with another man
- Been a male or female sex worker
- Engaged in sexual activity with someone who ever injected drugs not prescribed by a doctor or dentist
- Engaged in sexual activity with someone who was found to have HIV, Hepatitis B, Hepatitis C

I believe this undue caution is a discriminatory policy. It is based on emotion rather than science and further marginalises people in these groups. Back in 2021, in preparation for my Feast History Walks that year, I asked Will to offer blood. He explained to Life Blood staff that he was a single man, that he met their celibacy criteria, but was planning to have some safe sex fun at the gay sauna in the near future. Oh, he can be provocative! I'm surprised he didn't sport his 1970s 'How dare you presume I'm heterosexual' badge. They refused to take his blood and directed him to the refreshment bar to have a free cup of coffee. Wasn't that generous of the staff, Rainbow History Lovers? I didn't want to put him through this rejection again, so I didn't ask him to repeat this offer at the Port Adelaide Centre when he was preparing for our 2022 walk.

Let's now move eastward along St Vincent Street and, behold, we do indeed have a church. How very appropriate it should be on a street named after a saint. Casting your eyes eastward you will note a very fine cluster of buildings. There's the bold, geometric lines and patterns of Art Deco side by side with a fine nineteenth-century tower. Look at those classical columns and leafy volutes. Oh, I do appreciate a leafy volute! These are the Council Chambers and Town Hall of the City of Port Adelaide Enfield. As Will and I reside in the suburb of Sefton Park, this is our city!

'Passing' and 'St Paul's-on-Piles'
Church Place

Rainbow History Lovers, let's pause here in the shadow of 'St Paul-on-Piles' and have another tale or two. Official reports show in the nineteenth and early twentieth century numbers of Australian people assigned female as birth, mainly working class, lived their lives 'passing' as men. Many married women. It was only by chance their sex assigned at birth was discovered, at the time of their death, or during hospitalisation, for example.

Here's another paragraph from my dear friend Ian which I like:

> How did these people understand themselves? Were they nonbinary or transgender men? Were they lesbian or otherwise experiencing same-sex desire for other women? Or were they women taking advantage of the economic and social advantages afforded to men but not women in those times? Or some combination of these explanations?

The most celebrated case of a person assigned female at birth passing as a man in Adelaide's history is told in the pages of the Melbourne *Truth* in May 1925 with the sensational headline, 'O, Man Where is thy Victory – Woman Who Wooed a Woman'. William Hunter-Bailey lived and worked on the wharves at Port Adelaide for twenty years before he contracted rheumatic fever in 1923, and his 'deception' was discovered by a doctor. He was engaged to be married at the time 'to one of the Port's prettiest girls'.

William had appeared at 'the Port' one day many years before, 'and had worked in her dungarees down at the waterfront, as capably as any man.' The *Truth* elaborated:

> Sitting around the tar barrel she could tell the best of jokes and talk about the flappers in the approved 'man' style. She would tell of her flirtations, with as much embellishment as the others, and to her talks on lovemaking she would throw in a bit of what the others could not do – artistic, original blasphemy, for Bill was one of the best cussers, the most eloquent swearers, around the wharves.

William lived in a boarding house for wharf labourers. They did not drink or smoke and would often visit the Missions to Seamen for a yarn and a read. 'She took innumerable girls to the picture show and squeezed their hands with an ardour greater perhaps, than the known Port sheiks.' William went missing after leaving Adelaide Hospital, but according to the *Truth*, 'word was received at The Port that she is keeping up her deception, but now as a miner in West Australia'.

Rainbow History Lovers, how times have changed, thankfully for the better for transgender people. Although the path may not be easy there is surely much greater acceptance, even embrace of gender diversity in our community. And let's not forget our intersex community. I understand there is a least one person from the era of this story who was discovered to be intersex upon postmortem. As you are only too aware I use the term Rainbow to embrace our LGBTQIA+ family. It is so pleasing to see the transgender colours of white, light pink, and light blue incorporated into our Rainbow flag in 2018 and the intersex flag of yellow with a purple circle in 2021. As you know, one of my mottos is 'add another hue unto the Rainbow'. In this of course I am at variance with The Great Bard!

Rainbow History Lovers, let's make a few comments about St Paul's before we move on. This is the fourth church on this site. The current building celebrated its centenary in 2005, just in time for my Rainbow History Walk that year. Its history is celebrated with a Blue Heritage Plaque. Life in early Port Adelaide could be quite treacherous. It is recounted when St Paul's first opened in 1841, it was indeed built on piles to protect it from rising waters:

> the people went to service dry shod and unsuspicious. While it was proceeding, the water rose higher and higher, until it burst over an embankment which had been made for such a contingency, and by the time the service was concluded the church was surrounded by tidal waters, so that the out-coming people, could not get away. They were kept waiting in the cold west wind until Captain Lipson, the harbourmaster, sent boats to rescue them.

Indeed, at times townsfolk had to row boats to get about town.

There's another important reason to pause at St Paul's. At the time of my 2005 walk the incumbent rector was the lovely Ali Wurm, an out and proud lesbian. She was a speaker at a Feast Forum that year, titled 'Rainbow

Community Rainbow Communion', where the focus was building diverse Christian communities in which queer people are respected and celebrated.

Having just told the tale of William passing as a man, I think in a Christian denomination where the priests are predominantly males who 'frock up', it is rather nice to have a female rector who is an out and proud lesbian!

Ali was rector at St Paul's and then neighbouring St Bede's Semaphore from 2004 to 2011. Will well recalls attending a special showing of *Brokeback Mountain*, followed by a Q&A session, at the Semaphore Odeon Star Cinema which Ali had organised for her church community. In conversation with Ali, preparing for the 2022 walk, she spoke of the wonderful support she had received from the local church communities, but it was the conflict with the conservative church hierarchy which caused her to leave the parish. *The Sunday Mail* covered the story of Ali's departure. 'LESBIAN PRIEST IN LAST HURRAH', read the caption. 'Flanked by a drag queen lesbian priest Ali Wurm will today conduct a final service'. Of course, the drag queen was I! The article featured a gorgeous, coloured photograph of Ali giving me 'a leg up'. I did indeed attend the farewell service and spoke at the lunch which followed. You could feel the love in the room with Anglicans from all over town attending to support Ali. I dressed in my gala best. My luncheon topic was 'The falling dress standards of Anglican women: No frocks, no hats, no gloves, no parasols'. If I do say so myself, I was rapturously received!

The 2011 article concluded with this statement from the archbishop of the day, 'The Anglican Church of Australia maintains a traditional approach to human sexuality'. Rainbow History Lovers, I shall update you on the Anglican position on same-sex marriage, in some detail, on our Gay Bay Walk (pages 57-59). As always… more to look forward to!

Now, let's proceed down Church Street to Dale Street.

Women's Health Centres
Dale Street

Rainbow History Lovers, on that first 2005 Feast Walk we celebrated a twenty-first anniversary – that of the Dale St Women's Health Centre. If you cast your eyes opposite, you will note a rather charming two-storey building at number 56, which became the Dale St Women's Health Centre in 1984. One of its former incarnations was as the rectory for St Paul's, which makes a rather nice connection with our last stop.

On that occasion I was wearing my 'Shame, Fraser Shame' badge because only two days before we had remembered the thirtieth anniversary of the egregious dismissal of the pioneering Whitlam Labor Government on the 11th of November 1975. On the 2022 walk we celebrated the fiftieth anniversary of Gough's election in 1972 and the era of great social reform which he initiated. One of these reforms was the creation of a universal health system, Medibank. His government was also responsible for the establishment of community health centres and in particular women's community health centres. As one might expect, radical women from Women's Liberation were at the forefront of this movement, some of whom were lesbians who were also involved in the early Gay Liberation movement.

These radical women saw the health centres as being for women who were tired of attending unsympathetic or sometimes hostile male doctors. One of the goals put forward was 'to smash the patriarchy by Christmas'! The first centre was in the Sydney suburb of Leichhardt, affectionately known as 'Dykeheart' because it had become a popular residential area for lesbians. Here in Adelaide the women's movement organised a meeting and decided to apply for funding. They established an association and got their first grant in 1974 for capital works and operating costs.

Will remembers several prominent Adelaide radical lesbians, including the Jackson sisters Penny and Sally, approaching him for assistance to set up the accounting records, because he was working as an accountant at the time. The centre operated initially from the home of a doctor, followed by the Women's Liberation House and then finally from its own premises at Mary Street, Hindmarsh. The Mary Street Centre ran from 1976 to 1983. The approach was collectivist, holistic, and multi-disciplinary. Discussion groups were also held. Medical officers bulk-billed and offered long consultations. No single person had overall responsibility. There was a management committee with community involvement.

The 1980s saw the establishment of women's health centres in the central, northern, southern, and western districts, under the direction of the state government. Thus, Dale Street was opened in 1984. As with its forerunner Mary Street, it was chosen for its homely, non-clinical, non-threatening atmosphere. Then, the latter part of the 1990s saw the mainstreaming of services to create greater efficiencies, and women's health centres were amalgamated with community health centres in their regions.

And so, Dale Street Women's Health Centre moved across the road to these modern mainstream premises on the corner of Church and Dale Streets. Let's take a peek. 'Cedar Health Service. Inclusive domestic and family violence health service. South Australian Government Women's and Children's Health Network', the signage tells us. And look, stickers of the Rainbow, Transgender, Aboriginal and Torrens Strait Islander flags all prominently displayed! It's indeed a heartening sign of welcome and embrace, is it not, Rainbow History Lovers? Observe the wall art too, 'BECAUSE WE'RE WOMEN… THE SEEDS ARE PLANTED HERE. A PLACE TO COME AND GROW IN.'

The Federal Minister of Health and Aged Care in the first Albanese Labor Government, Mark Butler, whose office we have passed today, is promoting greater use of multi-disciplinary health teams, rather than relying solely on GPs. I'm sure these pioneering women of these women's health centres would applaud.

As we prepare to promenade down Dale Street to our last stop, cast your gaze on the modern building on the opposite corner next to the former Dale's Street Women's Health Centre. It's the Port Adelaide Library of the City of Port Adelaide Enfield, its architectural style very much in sympathy with its nineteenth-century neighbour, I think. I'm imbued with a sense of optimism when local government embraces our Rainbow Family overtly as the city library has done by requesting and sponsoring the 2022 Feast History Walk through its local history officer Cindy Crook. The City of Port Adelaide Enfield always flies the Rainbow flag at its chambers during Feast too, a very visible sign of support. You will also note the rather distinctive Greek Orthodox Church, The Nativity of Christ, across the road from the library. Now, here is another Christian religion which has not embraced same-sex marriage.

And so, let's continue our meander down Dale Street to our final stop. You will note the architecture of the street is rather varied with several two-storey stone dwellings similar to the former women's health centre intermingled with the modern. There are the imposing modern offices of the Australian Manufacturing and Workers' Union (AMWU) and look at the large, colourful signage indicating Port Adelaide Plaza and Port Mall just off Dale Street. They are both modern and expansive shopping centres. Oh yes, 'the Port' is a very busy shopping hub for the surrounding suburbs. I suspect this was once quite a fine residential street – well, the Church of England rector certainly lived here. Here's another church, St Mary's Catholic Church, complete with Blue Heritage Plaque. The Roman Catholic Church is another Christian denomination which remains opposed to same-sex marriage. One of my local sources told me when she was growing up in 'the Port' in the 1960s, her parents warned her about this street because it had become the red-light district. It must have fallen on hard times!

The Freemasons, AFLW, UCA and Climax!
Corner Dale Street & Commercial Road

Oh, Rainbow History Lovers, here we are at our final stop. Look across at the Masonic Temple and shops of 1928, one of the finest buildings in the street, with its striking Art Deco lines and Egyptian decorative features. It's quite grand, don't you think? Now, I'm sure you will be asking, 'Why are we finishing at the Freemasons?' Well, it's a fine building and I've indicated, time and again, how Ian, Will and I love to comment on streetscape.

Now, I don't know about you, Rainbow History Lovers, but I've always had my suspicions about the Freemasons with all their secrets and funny handshakes. It's male, deistic, and they wear regalia too. It is said Freemasonry dates back to the days of the construction of Solomon's Temple. Certainly, as artisans they were involved in the construction of castles and cathedrals in medieval Europe and passed on their crafts and rituals from one generation of artisans to another. By the eighteenth-century Freemasonry had become more of an honorary association. Mozart and Beethoven were Freemasons for example.

And many prominent folks are numbered in their midst: US presidents (Washington and the Roosevelts), SA governors, English kings (Edward VII, Edward VIII, George V and George VI), and South Australian Chief Justice Sir Samuel Way, who was the first Grand Master of Adelaide Grand Lodge established in 1884.

But are the Freemasons anti-gay or anti-woman? Looking at their mission statement, it would appear not so. We are told a Freemason:

- Seeks ways to share in building a better community
- Shows tolerance and respect for opinions of others and behave with kindness and understanding
- Practises charity
- Strives for truth and high moral standards

Do they define 'moral' in a narrow sense I wonder? Would polyamorists be welcome do you think, Rainbow History Lovers?

I was interested to note some fundamentalist Christian groups have information on their websites which condemns and criticises Freemasonry. They cite a nineteenth-century Grand Master Albert Pike as a 'notorious sodomite' and link the medieval Knights Templar with homosexual orgies and rituals involving urination on crucifixes. These fundamentalist Christian organisations run groups called 'Ex-Masons for Jesus' and claim even Ex-Masons may be under so much spiritual bondage they may be dysfunctional Christians. They also caution about allowing former Masons assuming leadership or teaching roles in the church. Even some mainstream Christian denominations, The Greek Orthodox and Roman Catholic Churches for example, are opposed to Freemasonry.

Well, the Freemasons are beginning to sound all right to me. I am a bit worried about the lack of women as members, so I thought I would approach the SA Grand Master with a revolutionary plan to bring them into line with modern values. I'm proposing they form a women's branch which could be called the Masonettes perhaps?

Rainbow History Lovers, I shall conclude with some important comments about the UCA and the AFLW. I do love an acronym! Don't you? Unlike my 2005 walk which focused on Freemasonry at the final stop, for the 2022 walk I gave Uniting Church of Australia (UCA) and Australian Football League Women's (AFLW) the final focus. As I always remind my loyal walkers:

> The walk will take between one and a half and two hours. If you are tight at the end, you are free to leave en route. But a warning. If you depart early, you will miss the climax and whoever wanted to miss a climax?

On doing locale research for the 2022 walk, I was taken by the striking bunting which flew from numerous flagpoles throughout 'the Port'. The flags, which depicted a young woman dressed in the Port Power Football Club uniform with the caption 'There's Herstory in the making', were celebrating the Port Power AFL Women's team, which had entered the competition for the first time in 2022. One of these flags was conveniently flying at this last stop. How fortuitous, Rainbow History Lovers! The team's captain is celebrated Portonian, Erin Philips, an out and proud lesbian. Indeed, the current banner which leads my walks depicts Erin giving her wife Tracey a passionate kiss at the AFLW awards when she was awarded Player of the Year in 2017. It's a picture from *The Advertiser* with the bold caption, 'SEALED WITH A KISS. PICTURE TELLS A THOUSAND WORDS ABOUT THE NEED FOR GAY MARRIAGE'.

There's also the Port Power Queer Squad which has been in operation for the last two men's and women's seasons. Their attendance at matches can be very visible with their Port Adelaide-themed Rainbow flag. AFLW held its first Pride Round in 2022 with all eighteen clubs participating. As usual women are leading the way. The men's AFL has still to hold a dedicated Pride Round with all clubs participating. Come on, boys! Get onboard!

Ah, the changing face of football! One of the listed events in the Rainbow History section of South Australia's History Festival 2022 program was even titled just that, 'The Changing Face of Football'. The exhibition was staged at both the Port Adelaide Visitor Information Centre, that lovely stone and red brick building I pointed out earlier (page 31), and at the library on Dale Street. Indeed, I was invited to the launch at the Visitor Centre. The program note read:

> The footy has traditionally been the place of beer, pies and the archetypical 'Aussie bloke'. More recently, we have seen stories of players 'coming out'. LGBTQI+ supporters and a women's league. As these themes become more common, stories of acceptance and resistance emerge. This display examines the history and the future of the game.

I then asked my walkers to cast their eyes across to the imposing nineteenth-century church which is the home of Port Adelaide UCA. It is a parish which is very embracing of our Rainbow Family. UCA is the Christian denomination which has consistently participated in Feast throughout its history. It's now in its twenty-sixth year! It's the Christian denomination in

Australia which leads the way in solemnising same-sex marriages. When I was doing my research, I was struck by the words on the church's noticeboard, 'GAY & TRANS KIDS WELCOME HERE. RELIGIOUS BELIEFS MUST NEVER OVERRULE HUMAN RIGHTS'. Well, what was the noticeboard message on the day of the walk? There, in bold capital letters was the message, 'PORT ADELAIDE WELCOMES DR GERTRUDE GLOSSIP'. You see one of my Gertrude Groupies, Paul Marsh, who is a prominent member of the parish, had arranged this. And of course, we all swooped across the road where my Gertrude Groupies insisted on being photographed with me before this wonderful signage!

Oh, Rainbow History Lovers, what a climax!

The Gay Bay: Nautical but Nice

Gertrude standing before the Glenelg Town Hall.

The Gay Bay: Nautical but Nice

Rainbow History Lovers here we are at the lovely seaside suburb of Glenelg, also affectionately known as 'the Bay'. To the Kaurna people, the traditional owners, Glenelg is Pathawilyangga. Doesn't Gay Bay have a wonderful resonance? These words were meant for each other. But should it be Gay Bay History Walk or Bay Gay History Walk? Which do you prefer?

You see, before the arrival of English colonists in 1836 this area had been the home to the Kaurna people for tens of thousands of years. In fact, they used it as a place of refreshment during long, hot summers. It was a meeting place for celebration, ceremony, and trade. And it was here the new English Governor John Hindmarsh landed, and just up the road read the proclamation for the province of South Australia on the 28th of December 1836. And here's part of the proclamation statement written by the first Colonial Secretary Robert Gouger (you'll hear from Gouger at the conclusion of the walk by the way, pages 74-75):

> It is also, at this time especially, my duty to apprize the colonists of my resolution, to take every lawful means for extending the same protection to the native population as to the rest of His Majesty's subjects, and of my firm determination to punish with exemplary severity all acts of violence or injustice which may in any manner be practised or attempted against the natives, who are to be considered as much under the safeguard of the law as the colonists themselves… promoting their advancement in civilisation, and ultimately, under the blessing of Divine Providence, their conversion to the Christian Faith.

Well, well. The language is certainly 'of the period'. The sentiments are interesting: 'equal protection under the law', 'advancement in civilisation', 'conversion to the Christian Faith'. I'm sure the latter two would not, and indeed should not, be in such a proclamation in 2023! As I penned this walk, the South Australian Parliament, at a special sitting on Sunday the 26th of March 2023, unanimously passed legislation which enshrines an Indigenous Voice to parliament. Despite the cold, wet weather, many people gathered on the steps of Parliament House and on specially constructed stands in North Terrace to witness this historic event. It has only taken 186 years! Better late than never!

Moseley Square
Moseley Square

Now, Rainbow History Lovers, cast your eyes about. There's the imposing 1936 marble monument, the Pioneer Memorial, which celebrates the centenary of the Province of South Australia and commemorates 'founding fathers' Wakefield, Gouger, Torrens, and Angas. And if we cast our Rainbow eyes beyond it, there's the jetty and sparkling sea of Holdfast Bay. To our left is quite a grand hotel. Please note the balconies. There's an amusing Rainbow story which occurred on the balcony of its former incarnation, The Pier Hotel, in 1976. But I'm going to tell you that at the conclusion of our walk (pages 74-76). I'm just whetting your appetite. One should always have something to look forward to!

Oh, look! There's the iconic Bay Tram which has its terminus here at Moseley Square. There's been a tram service to Glenelg since 1929. It replaced the steam trains which came right down Jetty Road to this terminus. More about the Bay Tram a little later (page 61).

But let's have a Rainbow tale before we move off. Cast your eyes across to that fine nineteenth-century building with its imposing tower. It's the former Glenelg Town Hall, designed by famous Adelaide architect Edmund Wright. Wright designed many notable buildings in Adelaide including its Town Hall, General Post Office, and the fabled Edmund Wright House in King William Street. This Wright building opened in 1877 as the Glenelg Institute, became the Town Hall in 1887 and remained so until local government amalgamations in 1997. It now houses the Bay Discovery Centre Museum, which is certainly worth visiting. It's a very visual history of Glenelg as a beachside resort. I adore the photographic images of beachgoers over the decades.

It was here in the grand hall in 1973 that a very celebratory event in Adelaide Rainbow history occurred. Picture the scene, Rainbow History Lovers, the very first Adelaide Gay Pride Week had commenced the day before, and here, on Saturday the 8th of September, a gay dance called 'Cosmos' was held. It was reported thus in the October edition of *Boiled Sweets*, the magazine of Adelaide's Gay Activists Alliance, the organisers of Gay Pride Week:

The Gay Bay: Nautical but Nice

There was much gyrating to the sound of Taxi by a fair crowd. Some street theatre was performed during the evening. The items were an attempt to highlight the main sources of our oppression: the family emphasising the sinfulness of sex and the enforcement of the blue boy/pink girl syndrome; the terrible sexist games of adolescence we play and are made to play; the church emphasising heterosexual marriage as the way of life; and our friend the psychiatrist with his little bag of tricks and cures. The final scene was a liberation scene in which SuperGay vanquishes the Agent of Repression, freeing his captives forever.

Well, well, Rainbow History Lovers, that's quite a message, isn't it? Those early Gay Liberationists could be quite serious don't you think? Incidentally, it was Will who penned that report. And even though the Gay Libbers were out and proud, they apparently had to be discreet about the nature of the dance. And so, it was booked as 'Cosmos Dance' with no reference to Gay Liberation and Gay Pride Week. You must remember, Rainbow History Lovers, until the emergence of Gay Liberation, most homosexual people lived hidden or at best discreet lives. There were still legal sanctions against male homosexual sex. I guess these early liberationists were learning how to be *out* and *proud*.

The grand hall was also used in the 1970s to hold Women's Dances on International Women's Day. There would be a march and fair during the day and then the dance here in the evening. And, of course, there were radical lesbians who were very much involved in both the Women's Liberation and Gay Liberation.

Now, let's move on to our next story. Follow me around the periphery of this lovely building with its fine stonemasonry to the verdant expanse beyond.

Colley Reserve: The Great Drag Race
Colley Terrace

Here we are, Rainbow History Lovers. Let's get a little perspective on the area by mounting this fine 1926 rotunda with its intricate iron lacework and stairs of marble. Just look at the high-rise apartments all around us. Thankfully they haven't built on this lovely green space. Of course, there was once a huge fun park, our own Luna Park with a Big Dipper roller coaster, along the foreshore. The giant water slide is a reminder of these fun glory days.

Let's focus on the green expanse. This is the site of the fabled Bay Sheffield annual footrace which began on Proclamation Day 1887. It was a hundred-yard dash with only male competitors and a first prize of fourteen pounds. Women did not compete until 1987. It only took one hundred years. Better late than never!

Now, speaking of the male/female binary, we know much greater attention has been given to the rights and recognition of transgender and intersex people by our Rainbow community in recent years. Indeed, our Rainbow acronym LGBTQIA+ embraces transgender and intersex people. As I have commented in our Port Walk (page 43) the Pride Progress Flag of 2018, which is most often flown nowadays, has added the transgender colours of white, pink and light blue, and black and brown to represent people of colour. More recently in 2021, a new design was created to incorporate the intersex flag of yellow with a purple circle. Oh, Rainbow History Lovers, one can never have too much colour. As you know, one of my mottos is 'Add another hue unto the Rainbow'.

Now, the rights of trans people to participate in sports have been receiving particular focus. In 2021, World Rugby banned trans feminine people who medically transitioned after a testosterone-based puberty from competing in women's elite events and subsequently World Swimming and World Athletes followed suit, in 2022 and 2023 respectively. In mid-2023, in a shift away from blanket bans, the Australian Sports Commission (ASC) updated their guidelines to restate their commitment to the 'spirit of inclusion' while being in line with the International Olympic Committee policies. You see, the ASC, being an Australian body, must comply with the with the Australian Sex Discrimination Act, which makes it illegal to discriminate, harass or victimise on the basis of gender and sex but it does provide an exemption for sports where safety risks and unfair advantages can be proven. The new ASC guidelines will approach each assessment on a case-by-case basis. Thankfully such restrictions are not imposed at the community level here in South Australia. The Education Department guidelines state, 'The goal for gender diverse and intersex children and young people is full participation in all types of sporting activity'.

Now, speaking of hundred-yard dashes, there is another story about dashing and Colley Reserve which goes back to the late 1940s. It was told to John Lee in one of his oral history interviews. In *Queen of the Walk*, I recounted the story of Bert Hines and his Lampshade Shop in Rundle Street where rather flamboyant camp parties were held. These gatherings came to the attention of police. As a result, a number of young men were charged with 'homosexual crimes' and sentenced to prison terms. In sentencing, Mr Justice Ligertwood stated, 'It must have come as a shock to the citizens of Adelaide to learn that there were centres of homosexuality in this city' and 'my duty is to carry out the law and to impose sentences which will act as a deterrent to others, who are minded to commit homosexual crimes'. Well, listen to the words of one of John's interviewees about some of the young men who attended Bert's parties and liked to dress in drag:

> They were all in drag – fluffing around and screaming. They would get on the tram and they were all dressed in frocks and hats and would go down to the beach. All those drag queens would be walking along the seafront where Luna Park is there and the hoodlums used to chase them and they would all go screaming and clattering up the street and jump on the tram.

Now, as with all oral history stories, we rely on the tellers' recall and interpretation. But it does sound as if these drag seafront frolics near Colley Reserve may not have been a 'one off'. Perhaps there was a certain daring and thrill in such an escapade – the dash and chase!

Let's move on, Rainbow History Lovers, by progressing down Augusta Street.

St Peter's and the Anglican Church of Australia
Torrens Square

As we approached our next stop, please note the streetscape which is rather modest compared to the high-rise apartments we have been viewing. Look at those single-storey 1960s flats on our right and the 1920s bungalows on our left. Now, cast your Rainbow gaze to that fine edifice before us. It is one of the historic buildings of Glenelg, St Peter's Anglican

Church. The site was chosen by William Light, the designer of the City of Adelaide. The first church was erected in 1851 and a second in 1883, which is the current rather fine building. Both were designed by, you guessed it, the architect of the Town Hall, Edmund Wright. This lovely gothic-style building boasts more than thirty stained-glass windows. The grand three-panelled stained-glass window above the high alter is particularly fine. I do adore the golden glow created when the eastern sun shines through this stained glass. It's quite... heavenly, really!

As you know, I can't resist a beautiful church and it always brings me to the issue of religion and attitudes to our Rainbow Family. The pamphlet 'Welcome to St Peter's Church' begins with 'A vibrant, welcoming and inclusive community'. Whenever I see the word 'inclusive' I am encouraged. I have covered the position of the Anglican Church of Australia in some detail in *Queen of the Walk*. Conducting same-sex marriage and the participation of women as clergy are now key indicators of embrace for me. This denomination still does not conduct same-sex marriages and only two of its twenty-three dioceses conduct blessings. The Diocese of Adelaide does not. However, twenty diocese including Adelaide, now ordain women priests. Adelaide has a woman bishop and Perth a woman archbishop. Encouragingly, this is putting paid to that concept of 'male, pale and stale'.

In 2022, Will was invited to speak at several Anglican forums, most notably at St Chads Fullarton, a few suburbs east of here. It was well attended and Will felt very welcome. The topic was '50 years after the death of Dr Duncan is the Rainbow Family embraced?' After the presentation *Queen of the Walk* proved popular too. The parish priest is a woman. She purchased a copy of course! It was so heartening to see a large, permanent posting on the front fence of the church, 'A community that openly and publicly supports LGBTIQ people'. Similarly, St Oswald's in nearby Parkside, offers this public embrace. And guess what, Rainbow History Lovers? The parish priest is none other than out, proud lesbian, the lovely Ali Wurm who you've just read about in 'Queering the Port' (page 43). Oh, I do love connections!

Taking a national Anglican sweep, Will recounts visiting two Anglican churches in Sydney while there for the 2023 Mardi Gras and World Pride celebrations. Now, there is something of a divide in the Australian Anglican Church between progressives and conservatives, the former embracing women clergy, for example, and the latter not. I suspect the progressives, given the opportunity, might well embrace same-sex marriage and the conservatives definitely not. One of the churches Will visited was historic St Stephen's in Newtown, a conservative parish in the conservative Diocese of Sydney. Will was dressed rather blatantly in Rainbow armbands and a '78er' T-shirt with badges such as 'How dare you presume I'm heterosexual'! I don't think he was trying to be provocative. Will reports a handsome, youthful priest was welcoming and engaged readily. Will was on his best behaviour and did not mention same-sex marriage either. Later in the day Will visited progressive Christ Church St Lawrence dressed in the same attire. The welcomer greeted him warmly and immediately enquired, 'Did you have a good time last night?', an obvious reference to the Mardi Gras Parade. They got into conversation and Will recounted his St Stephen's visit. The welcomer commented the conservative church may seem to be friendly and embracing but advised caution as they have an approach which he labelled, 'pray gay away'! And let's not forget the Anglican Diocese of Sydney, the largest and wealthiest in the country, donated a million dollars to the 'Vote No' campaign in the lead up to the same-sex marriage postal survey. Ah, we must be forever vigilant. The forces of reaction are ever-present. Let's leave our focus on religion and our Rainbow Family. Never fear, we shall return! And so, to a secular focus.

Rainbow History Lovers, we are going to make our way to Glenelg's main street that is Jetty Road. Which route shall we take? Nile Street or Sussex Street? Nile Street, I think not! You see, there's a modern supermarket with a huge carpark. I know we must have these modern amenities, but they're not very aesthetic, are they?

Before we proceed to Sussex Street cast your gaze southward to the far end of Nile Street and behold two rather distinctive structures, a nineteenth-century church building in the Gothic style and a tower in the Classical Italianate style. It's St Andrews by the Sea Uniting Church which we shall come to on our Jetty Road story (page 62). More to look forward to!

Sussex Street... without Zest
Sussex Street

So here we are Rainbow History Lovers in Sussex Street and from here I want you to case your Rainbow gaze northward. In the near distance, where Sussex Street meets Anzac Highway, is a cylindrical tower block, Atlantic Tower Motor Inn, which was part of the 1970s building redevelopment of Glenelg. I believe a cylindrical tower block was considered quite something back then, one might even dare to say 'ground-breaking'. The top floor boasted a revolving restaurant in which I've had the pleasure of performing. You see, a friend of Will's from the 1970s Gay Liberationist days, Richard, asked me to emcee his dear mother Leone's seventieth birthday party, which was held there in 1999. I was very keen to do this gig as Leone had always been so supportive of her gay son and his friends back in those days when many parents did not readily embrace the news their offspring were queer. Leone had also contributed several stunning outfits to my wardrobe. She loved 'flow and colour' and donated one of my faves which I wore on the 1999 Feast History Walks 'From Sacred to Secular: Queering the Dirty Mile'. Leone had retired to a commodious townhouse nearby, overlooking the Patawalonga Boathaven. Retiring to a beachside suburb such as 'the Bay' was, and is still, considered quite a thing for prosperous Adelaidean elders, I believe. The party was a lovely occasion and I, attired in cocktail black and pearls, was readily embraced by Leone's guests. This restaurant has been converted into a penthouse apartment. Ah... progress?

Sussex Street has an array of pleasant residences, some dating back to the nineteenth century. Here we are approaching Jetty Road. Oh, look! There's chic art shop The Changing Canvas and its neighbour Zest, which was a rather hip cafe until its closure in June 2023. Now this was a business operated by two charming gay men, David and Cameron, partners in business and in life. Cameron had held several successful art exhibitions here prior to 2001. In preparation for this tome, I had the pleasure of a chat with David. He recalled:

> We, perhaps recklessly, bought it and changed our lives forever. It has been a great move. We love Glenelg, always have, and have survived for nearly twenty-two years. We have always pitched our cafe to all ages and diversities. We have always aimed to create a space where anyone can feel confident and comfortable. We enjoy a strong local clientele. We have always been quietly out gay since we bought the business and we have always been supported by the local businesses. I spent several years as chair of the Jetty Road Traders Association, and was always treated with

respect and support. We have never been made to feel in any way uncomfortable. Glenelg remains a fairly conservative community, and I can't say there are any obviously queer spaces to socialise in the area. But there is an LGBTI population and we see many from time to time.

David explained how they had been strongly connected to the gay community through Feast, Adelaide Strikers Volleyball Club and attending venues, but operating a business seven days a week has meant this engagement has declined.

Will recalls attending a fun Rainbow New Year's Eve party early this century when David and Cameron 'lived over the shop'. Will has enjoyed calling in for refreshments when preparing for my Glenelg History Walks. I had the pleasure of entertaining walkers here after my 2022 Gay Bay Walk. Thus, I was rather devastated in late June 2023 to read via Facebook: 'Zest has closed its doors after a wonderful 22 year journey. Thank you to our loyal local support base'. Indeed, I'm sure there will be many loyal local Zest patrons who will be saddened by its closure and will miss the hospitality of David and Cameron.

Trams, Pride Parades, St Andrews and UCA
Jetty Road

Well, Rainbow History Lovers, here we are in the main street Jetty Road and right on schedule comes the fabled Bay Tram. There's an allure about a tram, or light rail as it is sometimes styled, which other motorised transport just does not have. You will note the trams are 'gayly' decorated with advertising and promotions. Did you know I have been emblazoned upon the Bay Tram? It was back in November 2012 when six major Adelaide events were being promoted on the Bay Tram. Feast Festival was one of them. There was my image, in a stunning red frock with matching hat and parasol, with long black gloves just for contrast. Of course, I was wearing the iconic 1960s sunshades which Will's aunt had passed on to me. I must have been the envy of many more glamorous Adelaide drag queens! And did you know Jetty Road might have become the parade route for our modern Pride March? You see, I had participated in Melbourne's Midsumma festival and had paraded down Fitzroy Street, St Kilda in their Pride March. Now, Fitzroy Street and St Kilda are Melbourne's answer to Jetty Road and Glenelg. So, I thought, why not do something similar here? As fortune would have it, I had been invited to write a regular fortnightly column for the Rainbow community magazine *blaze*. My very first column in March 2003 was titled 'LET'S MARCH' in which I wrote:

> Perhaps it is time we had a Pride Parade here in Adelaide. Of course the perfect time would be during 2003 Feast. This would have important historical resonances too. This September will be the 30th anniversary of the first Gay Pride March (the one and only I believe) held in Adelaide. Perhaps the original 73ers could lead the march much like the 78ers led the 20th anniversary Mardi Gras Parade... I think I shall make this one a personal crusade... We could retrace part of the 73 route and conclude with a party in Light Square perhaps. Or would a parade down seaside Jetty Road Glenelg cause something of a sensation?

Of course, I'm always drawn to the sensational! I do believe a Pride March down Jetty Road with a gala beachfront picnic to follow would have been quite the ticket.

Now, let's venture eastward along Jetty Road to Chapel Street. And here we have the fine buildings of St Andrew's by the Sea of the Uniting Church of Australia which I have already pointed out. The older Gothic-style building of 1859 was the original Congregational Church and the imposing building on the corner in the classical style is the subsequent church that opened in 1880. The Congregational, Methodist, and some of the Presbyterian Churches joined to form the Uniting Church of Australia (UCA) in 1977. And did you know way back in 1927 the Congregational Church was the first in Australia to have a woman as minister? And it was here in Adelaide too. Oh, we South Australians have led the nation in so many ways, have we not? Now, of all the Christian denominations in Australia I give the UCA the Rainbow tick of approval. I believe they have been the most embracing of our Rainbow Family. It is the denomination which has consistently participated and featured in Feast over the last twenty-five years. And of course, it ordains women. It is the only Australian denomination to embrace marriage equality and same-sex marriages have been conducted here at St Andrew's. Will delights in telling me of a UCA Easter service he attended in 2022 in which the minister's sermon celebrated a loving relationship between two women, American author Mary Oliver and her partner-in-life of more than forty years, Molly Malone Cook. It was beautiful and uplifting and a symbol of this denomination's preparedness to celebrate queer love.

Rainbow History Lovers, we're going to leave bustling Jetty Road and walk beside St Andrew's, down tranquil Chapel Street. How appropriate! Do observe the large, imposing, colourful sculpture 'Sesquipedalian Sea Squirt'. It honours an unusual species found in South Australian waters. It is designed to arouse curiosity and challenge one's perceptions. It certainly does mine. I just can't help it, can I? Always captivated, and indeed diverted at times, by streetscape! Let's continue down Chapel Street to High Street.

Art Deco, The Olives, Our Lady of Victories, and MacDonnell Lodge
High Street

Now, here we are in High Street. I have several streetscape delights to share with you here too. Oh, cast your Rainbow gaze at those gorgeous Art Deco-style houses on the corner of Olive Street. Look at the geometric detailing on those windows. Will and I adore Art Deco and I shall speak more about its association for him with the early Gay Liberation movement a little later (page 70). More to look forward to! And casting your gaze further down Olive Street you will observe a very fine two-storey mansion, The Olives, which is the oldest surviving mansion in Glenelg. It was built in 1867 and designed by, you guessed it, Edmund Wright. Oh, I could live here! It did have a period as a reception centre named Russell Court. Will recalls attending a glamorous wedding reception there in the 1970s. I can see stylish same-sex wedding receptions in such an establishment. Can't you, Rainbow History Lovers? However, unfortunately, we've left our run too late. You see, it's a private residence once more.

Now, westward ho down High Street and here's a building in the classical style which certainly captures our attention. Just look at those columns! It is imposing indeed. It is Our Lady of Victories Roman Catholic Church.

This is the third incarnation on this site. Indeed, we could say it's a reincarnation! The first was in 1869 and this, the third, in 1927. I am surprised it does not feature in the City of Holdfast Bay's booklet 'Historic Glenelg: a self-guided walk' as St Peter's and St Andrew's do. The Roman Catholic Church is surely one of the most conservative of the Christian denominations. It does not ordain women as priests and still requires all priests to remain single and celibate. I'm sure many priests honour these vows, but there are surely those who can't and don't. They are only human after all! Exposure of this is highlighted in the weighty tome *In the Closet of the Vatican: Power, Homosexuality, Hypocrisy* by Frédéric Marte. Perhaps same-sex communities, such as monasteries and convents, are conducive to same-sex activity, and indeed may be an attraction for those who are same-sex attracted. This denomination has certainly not embraced same-sex marriage. Unlike St Andrew's there've not been any same-sex marriages conducted at Our Lady of Victories. I've been told about a priest who served here. Same-sex attracted and humorously, indeed naughtily, known in some circles as 'Father Russell' because 'you could hear him in the bushes'. He did get into trouble with the law because of his same-sex activity, in a sylvan setting I believe!

Now, you will note the adjoining school, St Mary's Memorial School. This leads me to the topics of sex and religious discrimination. Under the Sex Discrimination Act of 1984 religious institutions can discriminate on the grounds of sexuality and can refuse to employ same-sex attracted people. As we know, in reaction to the success of marriage equality legislation, the conservative Federal Turnbull and Morrison Coalition Governments attempted to legislate a Religious Discrimination Bill, supposedly to protect religious freedom. As Lucas Lixinki, Professor of Law and Justice at UNSW stated, 'it was never about protecting religious freedom… it was about enshrining a right to discriminate against others' and that 'statement of belief clause' would allow people to make discriminatory statements on the basis of faith. He also noted a proposed amendment to prohibit the expulsion of students or the firing of teachers on the grounds of sexual orientation or gender identity, rather than providing protection, may have the effect of creating hostile education and work environments. Thankfully this legislation has been shelved. Under the more progressive Albanese Labor Government, let's pray it remains on the shelf!

Now, Rainbow History Lovers, look at that interesting building next door. It looks a little neglected, perhaps even unloved, doesn't it? I believe it is now a private residence. Note the pediment which brandishes, 'MacDonnell Lodge no.10 1860' together with the symbols of Freemasonry. We covered the Freemasons in our Port walk (pages 47-50). I think it's rather 'divine' a Roman Catholic Church and a Freemason's Lodge should be side by side, given that denomination's negative attitude to Freemasonry. Well, for a period from 1931 the Lutheran Church of Australia (LCA) held services here. Now, I have covered the importance and influence of this denomination in South Australian history in particular in *Queen of the Walk*. Still in 2023, women are not ordained and same-sex marriages are not conducted, my markers of progressive or conservative religious denomination, as you well know. I've told you often enough haven't I?

Rainbow History Lovers, let's continue on our journey westward down High Street to Moseley Street. Look at that distinctive redbrick 'period' building on the corner. Is there a streetscape story here? Come on, let's find out.

ECH, Charles Jury, College Street, and St John's Row
Moseley Street

So here we are in Moseley Street. Now, if you cast your gaze across to the two buildings on the corner you will observe two very different styles of architecture. It is this varied design which makes Glenelg's streetscape so interesting. There is the distinctive 1923 redbrick building, originally named Kilwinning Flats, at the time being considered a modern form of accommodation in the suburbs. Oh yes, can't you picture the scene? Myself as a 1920s flapper, residing in one of these modern flats, doing the Charleston at Town Hall, taking an esplanade stroll, followed by a dip in the ocean, then catching a train, and later a tram into town. Truly *Gert by Sea*!

On the opposite corner, the ECH ten-storey modern tower block, Manson Towers, is quite a contrast. ECH was established in 1964 as Elderly Citizens Homes SA and is now rebadged Enabling Confidence at Home. It has many independent living residences throughout the city and suburbs. It has made a considerable focus of supporting our Rainbow Family and was the first aged care provider in South Australia to receive the Rainbow Tick accreditation from Rainbow Health Australia. It has a designated LGBTI Connect Team whose role is to support Rainbow elders. The team has featured on the Bay Tram too. The Connect Team offers regular outings. The activities are quite varied. For example, I conducted a tour of the South Australian Museum's award-winning Rainbow exhibition 'It's In Our Nature: A Queer Trail of the Museum'. I've also conducted this tour for ECH staff on two occasions. ECH also sponsored a very important oral history project, in association with Oral History Australia SA/NT and the State Library, in which volunteers recorded oral histories of Rainbow elders to create a permanent record of their stories. These are housed at the State Library and are an invaluable resource. Will was an interviewer in this project which, sadly, was interrupted by the COVID-19 pandemic. ECH has been both a major partner and support partner of Feast Festival over many years. It has supported my walks and the wonderful exhibition 'Daring to be Different', which showcased the lives of Rainbow elders at the Migration Museum in 2019. In association with the State Theatre Company of South Australia, ECH sponsored a series of theatre workshops for Rainbow elders. These workshops culminated in the memorable Feast 2022 presentation 'The Rainbow Monologues' written and performed by eleven elders. Will of course was one of them!

ECH is a true exemplar of the embrace of Rainbow elders, some of whom come from a generation when folk chose to remain closeted or at least discrete, because being out and proud was not easy. And as Will likes to remind me, at an international conference on ageing held in Prague in 2012, he took to the floor and reminded the packed auditorium, 'We, the first Queer Out Generation, are now entering our Third Age. We *will* and we *won't* take things lying down'! Like my good self, doesn't he have a way with words?

Rainbow History Lovers, before we move on, I'd be remiss if I did not mention another Aged Care Provider and another grand house of Glenelg. Indeed, they are linked. Named Kapara (Kaurna for 'by the sea'), this house was designed by leading Adelaide architect George Soward of Beehive Corner fame. It is a little further south down Mosley Street at number 80 and it's now an expansive residence for seniors run by Aged Cottage Homes (ACH). I've even had the pleasure of conducting a Rainbow History Walk for ACH staff. At the heart of this five-acre property, is the fine 1890s house, built for prominent citizens George and Elizabeth 'Betty' Jury. It was at this address that their sons Charles and George were born and grew up. Charles and George served in World War I and both were wounded in action in 1915. Charles survived. George did not. Their names appear on the Honour Board in the Town Hall building. How fitting then that Kapara should have become a treatment centre for returned servicemen in 1919. It was renamed Anzac Hostel.

Now I mention the Jurys, not just because of their fine house, but because Charles is one of Glenelg's 'gay sons'! And I'm sure the City of Holdfast Bay would wish me to honour him thus! I tell Charles's story in some detail in *Queen of the Walk*. Again, let me whet your appetite with just a snippet. Charles became an academic and noted poet. In 1941, he wrote what was probably the first published depiction of male homosexuality in Australian poetry, the verse drama *Icarius*. It was described by distinguished Adelaidean John Bray as 'a play dealing with homosexual passion in a bitterly hostile world' in an Adelaide 'officiously blanketed in unctuous puritanism'. Brave heart and courage Rainbow History Lovers!

Now, let's move on. We're going to progress down a few back streets now. These will lead us back to the seafront. Oh, the very thought of sea breeze is most enticing, isn't it?

And so down College Street we go. As we progress, cast your gaze at the two rather fine Victorian terraces at numbers 3 and 5. In the 1870s, number 5 was the home of the South Australian Premier John Colton. In the 1960s both houses were styled College House Private Hotel in an era when Glenelg was very much sought after as a holiday resort for families. Private hotels did not serve alcohol. Opposite these terraces is another interesting building which was the coach house of a fine resident in Moseley Street. Oh, isn't Glenelg a historical and architectural treat? But wait, there's more to come.

Now, around the corner we go into St John's Row. This streetscape is now quite varied with the rear view of some fine seafront mansions and modern high-rises. Many of the mansions fronting South Esplanade kept beautiful summer gardens bordered by St John's Row, which was a service lane. These nineteenth-century mansions would have had long drops at the bottom of the garden and the night cart would have come down this lane to service them. Fortunately, the days of long drops and night carts are long gone! Oh, just imagine having to dash to the bottom of the garden through a strong sea breeze to answer the call of nature after dark!

Let's continue down this service lane. Now, cast your eyes to that terrace row on our left at numbers 14 through 17. A rather famous South Australian lived at number 16 in his youth. Whom do you think that might be, Rainbow History Lovers? It was none other than Lionel Logue, speech therapist to King George VI. I'm sure you all viewed the fascinating movie *The King's Speech* in which Logue was played by noted Australian actor Geoffrey Rush and the King by Colin Firth. As you can see, there's much notable history down here at 'the Bay'. Let's now proceed to the seafront and have a gay tale, shall we?

Encounters, Parties, Mansions and Childhood Memories
South Esplanade

Here we are on South Esplanade with the panoramic coastline of Holdfast Bay. Let's stroll southward along the Esplanade a little way. You will note a modern building right on the seawall where Broadway meets the seafront. It now houses The Broadway Kiosk and public lavatories. Well, those modern things which I call 'expelaloos'! There used to be a proper lavatory block with a urinal there, a popular meeting spot for gay men. I simply must share one of my favourite John Lee quotes about urinals, which I have used on so many of my walks and in *Queen of the Walk*. Unashamedly, I quote again:

> They were designed in the nineteenth century as a public solution to what had hitherto been a largely private matter. The introduction of rows of urinals was an imaginative solution to the problem of mass male urination – but they also happened to be very conducive to the casual glance, the discreet eye contact, the wordless, covert pick-up operation... Before the Second World War, beats in Adelaide provided many homosexual men, probably the overwhelming majority, with the only outlet for their homosexual desires and sociable contact with like-minded people.

Thus, the lavatory block here on the South Esplanade became well-known and visited. A mature gay couple, denizens of Glenelg since the

1970s, recall how well patronised the area around the Broadway lavatories was as a meeting place. It was easy to park, to stroll and to 'relieve' oneself if necessary. With laughter they told of a hearse which was often seen parked or 'patrolling' the area. They recall how popular the surrounding lawn area was for sunbathing, with many men luxuriating on towels. It sounds like a summer paradise doesn't it, Rainbow History Lovers?

David, a longtime activist friend of Will's, had a similar story to tell. He told of coming to live in Adelaide in 1967 and moving to Glenelg in 1971. Do you think Glenelg may have been a bit of a 'gay ghetto', Rainbow History Lovers? Here is his account of 'the scene' on South Esplanade at Broadway at that time:

> During that year [1971] it was my custom on Sunday evenings after dinner to walk down to the seafront and amble south from the jetty towards Broadway. If there was someone standing there pretending to admire the sea or the sunset it was a good sign that the beat was working. I never had sex on the premises – risky – so we went elsewhere. Several years later [mid 1970s] I heard of a friend of a friend who was arrested by police late one night with several other people having sex inside the lavatory. He paid Pam Cleland to take up his case and happily heard no more.
>
> If in a car one would park in the adjacent car park and see who turned up. In the evenings, especially in Winter, it was quite deserted – one could safely assume anyone there was doing the beat. Sometimes one would get out of one's car and do a short walk along the seafront and see if the other person followed. Or else one would drive off slowly, south down the esplanade, to see if the other car followed. Then it was a matter of stop and start, perhaps flashing headlights – always move for move – until a final stop when someone might get out and have a chat through the car window. 'Got anywhere to go?' Or sometimes the other person got nervous and drove off fast.

David remembers one particular encounter, which he found, and still finds, rather humorous:

> I recall that we drove back to my place in Rose Street and when we tumbled into bed found that we were both wearing identical

blue Paisley-patterned jockettes. Jockettes were fashionable for 'young' men in those days. The last time we met, several years ago, I reminded him of this but he did not remember. But by then it was almost fifty years ago!

What a delightful memory, Rainbow History Lovers! Ah, a sense of humour is so important in life. Fifty years on, would you remember an anonymous amorous encounter where you were both wearing identical underwear? Would that moment have been captured by an exclamation of 'snap!'?

Certainly, some of John Lee's interviewees remember this encounter spot well. 'You couldn't get in there sometimes; it was unbelievable. But they took it down because it was just too active.' Another said, 'There was only the party scene or the beat scene'.

So, let's now explore the Glenelg party scene of yore, shall we? Strolling northward along the Esplanade we come to number 18A, Shoreham Apartments, which was built in the 1930s. What a fine example of Art Deco architecture! Don't you adore those waterfall windows? It goes without saying seafront buildings should have waterfall windows, don't you think? Will tells me under the influence of John Lee, it was de rigueur for their Gay Liberation set to embrace all things Art Deco and the works of Stephen Sondheim. Oh, they were a toney lot. Now, several of John's interviewees spoke of parties down here at Glenelg. One recalled arriving in Adelaide aged twenty-one from the country in the 1930s. A friend took him to a party in a flat at Glenelg where there were six people in attendance. 'But that was a big party in those days,' he explained. Another said, 'In those days everything was very under the lap', and 'You couldn't be picky. You had to stick together.' There are stories of police raiding parties. Another told of a Glenelg party where there was a pianola and they 'got full on wine'. I suspect this was an era when the drinking of wine rather than just beer might have been considered rather daring. I like to think parties such as these may have taken place in Art Deco flats such as Shoreham Apartments.

Rainbow History Lovers, let's proceed a little further northward and stand before these two fine buildings Stormont at number 14, and Albert Hall at number 16. Will recalls coming down from the country for family holidays in the late 1950s and early 1960s and staying at number 14, at the time called St Olaves I believe. Glenelg was certainly a summer holiday resort for country folk and some of these old residences had been converted into guesthouses. Both these are again private residences and in very fine form too. There was a gracious residence at number 13, which became Glenelg's first seafront high-rise, where famed Australian aviator Jimmy Melrose lived with his mother. Jimmy is one of Glenelg's most famous sons. The verdant expanse near the jetty is named Jimmy Melrose Park with an impressive interpretive sign which celebrates his aviation achievements. It notes he had a close relationship with his mother and named three planes in her honour. Tragically, he died in a plane crash aged twenty-two. Jimmy was described as handsome, blond and six-foot-tall. Casting my Rainbow lens, I ponder how Jimmy's life might have unfolded had he survived his crash.

And just a few doors down at numbers 6 and 7 is another grand edifice, Seafield Tower. It is state heritage-listed and dates from 1876. It comprised two self-contained summer residences of noted South Australians Sir Henry Ayers and Sir Thomas Elder. The tower in between was shared. Sir Thomas was a bachelor. I'm always fascinated when very wealthy, prominent men of the nineteenth century remained bachelors. What does your Rainbow lens make of this? Again, Will has a childhood memory of number 6, the northern residence. By the 1960s it had been subdivided into apartments which were owned by a family friend. As a boy from the country, Will loved to visit and recalls the excitement of clambering up the stairs of the tower and viewing the seascape from the top.

Water Sports
South Esplanade

On my very first Gay Bay History Walk, as part of Lifesaving World Championship Adelaide 2018, I was keen to have some water sports stories. Luckily there was a lifesaver story from the John Lee oral histories. I certainly didn't want to give lifesavers a bad name, but I could not resist telling this tale.

It was at a party after a ball at the University of Adelaide when Glenelg lifesavers arrived and:

> pushed their bloody way into the joint and started to make fun of all the bloody queens in drag. About six of them. Jan Hillier

went to the door on her own and pushed the bloody lot of them off and two of them were ready to belt her up. She hit one of them in the face, thud, and laid him out and the others picked him up and fucking ran off. She was incredible.

Jan gained quite a reputation in the Adelaide camp scene in the 1960s. I do so enjoy that image of the bold lesbian taking on the macho, muscle-toned lifesavers, punching and laying one out.

Wouldn't it have been so exciting if some surf lifesavers had come out at the 2018 World Championship, Rainbow History Lovers? I am not aware that any did. They could have joined the Gay Bay History Walk too!

Now, as you know, Rainbow History Lovers, Will and I place great emphasis on visibility and the importance of coming out and declaring one's sexuality and gender identity. 'The Personal is Political' was one of the favourite catch-cries of 1970s Gay Liberationists. It is significant when prominent people come out. When sporting stars do so, given the prominence of sport in our Australian culture, it can have a very positive effect, especially for young people coming to terms with their identity. It is even more significant if they do so while still competing at the elite level. We have a number of out water sports Olympians who have done so. Craig Rogerson came out publicly prior to diving in the 1996 Summer Olympics, Mathew Helm in 2004, and Mathew Mitcham in the 2008. Mitcham, just twenty at the time, was one of only ten openly gay Olympians at the Beijing Games. Given there were nearly eleven thousand competitors, that's only 0.0009 percent of the Olympians. Recalling the old 'one-in-twenty' rule, which I consider conservative anyway, there would have been over five hundred queer athletes at these Olympics! I think these stats speaks *volumes* don't you, Rainbow History Lovers? Matthew has starred in our Feast Festival too. He was Ambassador for the 2014 festival and performed his show *Twists and Turns*. The full-page image of him dressed only in swimming togs with a ukulele in hand is indeed most alluring!

Swimmers Daniel Kowalski and Ian Thorpe both came out after retirement from competition. Kowalski, in 2010 aged thirty-five, publicly announced he was gay and said he had been inspired by the coming out of Welsh rugby star Gareth Thomas. Perhaps most significant was the coming out of Ian Thorpe. Ian shares the Australian record for the most Olympic gold medals with five wins. He was Young Australian of the Year in 2000. For years there were rumours about his sexuality. Finally, after years of public denial, in 2014 aged thirty-one, he came out in a very public way. It was during a televised interview with the prominent TV personality Michael Parkinson in which he said, 'I hope it makes it easier for others now, and even if you've held it in for years, it feels easier to get it out.' Well, good on you Ian. I think it does illustrate 'coming out' is not always easy, perhaps especially for elite sportsmen, but the more people of prominence do so the easier it will become for all.

As I commented at our Colley Reserve stop (page 56), transgender people's participation in elite sports is very topical. In 2022, World Aquatics (then called Fédération Internationale de Natation or FINA), the world governing body for aquatic sports, effectively banned trans feminine swimmers from elite competition if they began medical transition after the onset of a testosterone-based puberty. The concept of an open gender category is currently under consideration.

On a community level, I must honour another Australian, Bobby Goldsmith (1946 to 1984), who swam in the very first international Gay Games in San Francisco in 1982. He won an amazing seventeen medals. Bobby died in 1984, and was the first person in New South Wales to be publicly recognised as having died from an AIDS-related illness. The Bobby Goldsmith Foundation, which provides practical, emotional, and financial assistance to people living with HIV and AIDS, is named in his honour. Michael Kirby is a patron and Ita Buttrose a life member of the foundation. In relation to sports, Gay and Out Games have done a power of good in challenging sporting stereotypes and demonstrating queer folk 'do sport' and do it well. Individuals and teams from Adelaide have participated over the years. Adelaide has hosted the national Gay Gaymes twice, in 1995 and 2001. Sydney hosted the international Gay Games VI in 2002. Darwin hosted the Asia Pacific Outgames in 2014. Will has competed on a number of occasions in a number of sports and even medalled in sprint triathlon twice! An integral aspect of the games is the cultural festivals held. Indeed, I have performed while Will has competed. At the 2001 Adelaide Gaymes I conducted a Rainbow History Walk while Will competed in the tennis. At the Sydney Games I conducted my fabulous 'Wild Sex' walk at the fabled Taronga Zoo while Will cycled. I love the original name of the Adelaide group, founded in 1982, SAGSAA – South Australian Sports and Arts Association. Ah, the fusion of art and culture with sport!

Now, Rainbow History Lovers, cast your Rainbow gaze across the golden sands. Can't you just picture the scene, Beach volleyball here at Glenelg when Adelaide hosts the Olympic Games at some point in the future? What fun it would be! Of course, you know Sydney 2000 Gold Medal Beach Volleyballer Natalie Cook is a member of our Rainbow Family. She is married to another beach volleyballer Sarah Maxwell. Now, I know marriage is not for everyone, especially those old 1970s Gay Liberationists like Will, but it is important that it is available to all, no matter one's sexuality or gender identity. And it really facilitates coming out. 'Hello, I'm Natalie and this is my wife Sarah'. How easy and respectable is that?

Now, we are going to continue northward on our seaside promenade to our finale. We have done a walking loop as we shall arrive back at our starting point, the Pioneer Memorial, Moseley Square.

Stop the Waves! Climax!
Moseley Square

Here we are back at Moseley Square. Indeed, we have 'been round the Bay for a bob' as the saying goes. There's the jetty, the Town Hall, the 1936 monument, and the Stamford Grand Hotel on the site of the former Pier Hotel. You will note the balconies, which were a particular feature of the Pier Hotel. It was on one balcony Premier Don Dunstan performed a 'miracle' in 1976. You see in 1975, South Australia achieved Gay Law reform, which decriminalised male homosexual activity, the first jurisdiction in Australia to do so. A fundamentalist clairvoyant predicted an angry God would create a tsunami that would sweep in from Glenelg and destroy the city of Adelaide as punishment. And so, Don came down to Glenelg and stood on the balcony as an act of defiance, and as a symbol of solidarity and support for the legislation. Don was going to 'stop the wave' if necessary. Of course, it was a publicity stunt but one which pleased and delighted many of Adelaide's citizenry.

Rainbow History Lovers, as I have mentioned, Robert Gouger, one of the 'founding fathers' of the colony of South Australia, is honoured on the

Pioneer Memorial. I concluded my very first Feast History Walk in 1997 by quoting Gouger:

> Upon the importance of maintaining a balance between the sexes, however, it is impossible to speak too strongly; and it can only be adequately felt, perhaps by a person who had resided in a country where the proportion of females to males is fearfully small. Crimes of the most heartrending as well as the most abhorrent kinds are constantly occurring in such places, and offences for which the last punishment is awarded in England, are committed without the dread of such a result. From such horrors the province of South Australia is yet free, and perseverance in the present plan will doubtless keep it so.

I then told those History Lovers, 'Well, if Gouger were here today to see this wonderful celebration of Lesbian and Gay culture, I think he would be sadly disappointed his plan had failed!'

You will note my words 'Lesbian and Gay culture'. Of course, I would say 'Rainbow culture' today. Back in 1997 'Rainbow' was not so widely used. Indeed, that very first Feast Festival was styled 'Adelaide Lesbian & Gay Cultural Festival'.

Rainbow History Lovers there's just one more maritime tale I simply must share with you. Let's cast our eyes seaward to the horizon and image it's 1802. What would we see? Of course, the vessel HMS Investigator under the command of noted English explorer Matthew Flinders, who is acknowledged as the first European to circumnavigate the Australian continent. The Flinders Ranges, Flinders University of South Australia and Flinders Chase on Kangaroo Island are named in his honour. He'd share some earlier east coast explorations with another noted maritime explorer George Bass of Bass Strait fame. Now here is an excerpt from a letter by Flinders to Bass:

> There was a time, when I was so completely wrapped up in you, that no conversation but yours could give me any degree of pleasure; your footsteps upon the quarter deck over my head, took me from my book, and brought me upon deck to walk with you... but your apparent coolness towards me, the unpleasant manner you took to point out my failings, roused my pride and cooled my ardour... And yet it is not clear to me that I love you entirely;

at least my affection for Wiles reaches farther into my heart – I would take him into my skin with me.

Well, well Rainbow History Lovers that is some love letter, don't you think? Is it simply indicative of a nineteenth-century bromance or is it something more? Those male maritime navigators would have spent months together at sea with no female company. Historian Garry Wotherspoon has noted that, had the letter been written by a woman we would have no doubt what sort of relationship it was, the hope and expectation it contained, and that we would probably confidently presume a sexual component. What would Gouger has made of it do you think?

Now, returning to contemporary times, as I was concluding my 2022 History Festival walk with my Don Dunstan and Gouger stories, I became aware of an interjector who was loudly expressing anti-gay sentiments. He was a youthful man of robust build, and he became quite intrusive. My loyal Gertrude Groupies dealt with him in the best non-violent style. They drowned him out with sustained, enthusiastic applause! Outnumbered and deterred, he moved off. Oh, Rainbow History Lovers, thank goodness he was alone. What if there had been a group of them? It was a powerful reminder the forces of reaction are always with us and the importance of telling our stories in our own way.

So, thank you, Rainbow History Lovers, for joining me on this Gay Bay History Walk through the streets and along the foreshore of this charming and historic seaside suburb. And let us remember it was a place for celebration, ceremony and trade for the Kaurna people for tens of thousands of years before the arrival of British colonists in 1836.

Coastal Rainbow Tales

Gertrude overlooks Estcourt House and the Tennyson Dunes.

Rainbow History Lovers, I trust you have enjoyed our Port and Bay walks. Now, there are numerous coastal tales and events along the coastline of The Gulf of St Vincent, stretching from Mudlangga or Lefevre Peninsula, which, as you have learned, always looks rather phallic to me, all the way down the Fleurieu Peninsula, which looks rather like a foot, home to the Ngarrindjeri, Kaurna and Peramangk peoples. Fleurieu sounds rather French, doesn't it? It's undoubtedly a legacy of those nineteenth-century French explorers from the era when European powers were seeking colonies abroad.

My research took me back to browsing through all my old Feast Festival programs. From the early days there was always a tourist section to whet visitors' appetites to explore some of the delights of our city and surrounding areas. Beaches have featured consistently. There is one particular paragraph which has been used again and again over the years. I find it rather enticing, even exciting, so here it is:

> Adelaide's pristine beaches stretch forever. Start at Semaphore, the dyke paradise beach for great swell, cruise Escort [sic] Beach, catch a tram to historic Glenelg. Make your way to the most beautiful nude beach you will ever come across, Maslins [sic] Beach or motor down to Middleton and Boomers surf beaches.

I'm just a little disappointed they did not start at Outer Harbor, our phallic tip.

Now, Rainbow History Lovers, this really is a coastal cruise, not a History Walk, as we zoom down the coast and lightly touch on highlights and locations.

Coastal Cruising

So here we are at Outer Harbor. As you discovered in our Port Walk, Outer Harbor is Adelaide's deep seaport. It is here those enormous cruise liners of the twenty-first century now berth. I wonder if the majority of the stewards are gay men as of yore and if they have the opportunity to explore gay Adelaide while in port? Or indeed if gay Adelaideans seek them out? The location does have a rather remote feeling, doesn't it? I sense one would really only visit to board, disembark or greet arrivals. Oh, look! There's the Outer Harbor Railway Station, quite a distinctive redbrick structure built in 1926. As one walks up to the platform there is a fine wall painting of indigenous art with the Kaurna greeting 'Ninna Marni'. It is in this vicinity the rather grand Missions to Seaman Lakeman Institute, which you learnt about in 'Hello Sailor' (page 26-27), stood until destroyed by fire in 1992.

Let's proceed on our coastal cruise. As we progress down this coastal road, Lady Gowrie Drive, you will note the rather modern coastal housing development of North Haven. But, buoy ahoy, I see a jetty (or pier) in the distance. Let's keep going. Here we are at Largs Bay and just look at that imposing three-storey building, The Largs Pier Hotel. It opened in 1882 on the same day as the Largs Bay Railway and Pier. Largs Bay became the primary port of call for those immigrating to South Australia and many would have spent their first night at the Largs Pier Hotel. I've read it has a tradition of live music performances and Aussies icon Jimmy Barnes has such fond memories of performing here he wrote a song titled 'Largs Pier Hotel'. Peering through the windows it looks very well-maintained and patronised.

Now, Rainbow History Lovers, I am fascinated by the 'architecture' of public lavatories. This coastline is dotted with them. I sent Will on field work of course. He is so diligent he visited each one, both by day and after dark, from Largs Bay right down to Seacliff. I was interested to know if traditional lavatories had survived or if they had been replaced by those awful 'expelaloos'. I was heartened to learn most of the traditional facilities had survived and most male lavs had good-sized... urinals too! He reported only two expelaloos, both of which abutted a kiosk. One is located at the fabled Broadway at Glenelg which you learned about on our 'Gay Bay' walk. Will took particular note of detailed signage, with municipal logos, stating opening and closing times. For the city of Port Adelaide Enfield closure is 9 pm in Summer and 6 pm in Winter. For Charles Sturt it is 8:30 to 10:30 pm in Summer and 6:30 to 8:30 pm in Winter. Summer is October to March and Winter April to September. On his May after-dark fieldwork after 8 pm Will found all the lavatories still open, well almost. He had just used the facilities at the Grange Jetty lavatory when security arrived to do the lock up. 'Just made it in time,' Will quipped… gayly! The worker politely explained they lock up because folk 'make a mess and break bottles'. Hmm! That's the official rationale, is it? I have a theory it may be to discourage after-dark 'amorous activity', of gay men in particular! Rainbow History Lovers, I do hope you enjoyed our 'wee loo interlude' and my rationale for it!

But let's continue our journey south along our coastal road which is now styled Esplanade. Ah, another jetty in sight. And here we are at delightful Semaphore.

Semaphore and Seaside Feast

Now, the Rainbow community has quite an association with the suburb of Semaphore, picturesquely described in the Feast program as 'dyke paradise beach'. To the best of my knowledge and investigation Adelaide does not have Rainbow ghettos as such, but from the 1980s Semaphore became a favoured dwelling location for many lesbians. My good friend Helen Bock recounted how she, and others, were attracted to Semaphore. It was during the premiership of John Bannon whose South Australian Labor Government implemented a low-income housing scheme for single women who were over thirty years of age and employed. There was a narrow salary and housing-loan range. At that time there was a good supply of affordable housing stock in Semaphore and surrounding suburbs. This had the effect of attracting lesbians who worked in the arts in particular.

Semaphore did not quite have the reputation of tonier seaside suburbs such as Grange, Henley Beach, Glenelg, and Brighton. And so, a lesbian community developed. Helen was one of those attracted to this housing scheme. She explained the social fabric of Semaphore was quite diverse, with progressive folk of left-leaning political persuasion, Indigenous families, and mental health hostels. It was an accepting community, Helen says, with 'no lesbian aggro'. Helen also told of a period in the 1990s when a lesbian couple managed The Semaphore Hotel. Lesbians visited as a result and some locals saw it as a 'lezzo bar'. Helen worked in the bar for a period and recalls birthday parties and 'The Fabulous Semaphore Guitar Band', an all-lesbian band of which she was a member, playing on a number of occasions.

As we learned on our Port Walk the women's theatre, Vitalstatistix (pages 38-40), in Nile Street Port Adelaide was established at this time and Helen, and other lesbian Semaphore denizens, including Margie Fischer, Roxxy Bent, and Ollie Black, were very involved with 'Vitals'.

Thus, it is no surprise when Feast was established in 1997, Helen and Margie were two of four original Artistic Directors and Semaphore featured in the program. The 1998 program notes read:

> Sappho's at Semaphore: Interstate and South Australian lesbian poets read their work at the perfect setting of Melinge's Cafe by the sea at Semaphore.

For the 1999, 2000, and 2001 festivals 'Seaside Feast' was presented:

> Seaside Semaphore and Port Adelaide, only 20 minutes from the city, are hubs of the lesbian and artistic community. For one very special weekend Semaphore and the Port celebrate Feast. Today Semaphore takes pride in being a vibrant, safe and colourful seaside community built on a history of diversity, harmony and involvement.

A veritable feast of Semaphore treats was presented over these years, including the Corinthian Singers (at St Bede's Church Hall), 'The Long Lunch' (with Feast specials and entertainment at participating cafes on Semaphore Road), 'Love in the Afternoon' (a Writing Live event at The Lovin' Spoonful Café), 'Passions – All Sorts' (5 brilliant interstate writers at Corfu Restaurant) and '3 Fruits by the Sea' (a live music feast on The Deck of the fabulous Semaphore Palais).

In 2003 'Seaside Feast at Semaphore' returned with fabulously diverse offerings: beach blanket bingo, a drag sand sculpture competition, 'Sisters in Crime' at Pathfinders Bookshop, Pink Parents Picnic, Fairies at the Beach and beach volleyball. The day culminated with the 'Palais Meltdown', 'a top night of non-stop musical celebrations' at the fabulous Semaphore Palais on the foreshore.

Oh, Rainbow History Lovers, I can feel the Rainbow vibe as I write! Why, oh why, did I not attend? The very mention of the Palais brings forth a Will memory. You see the only marriage he ever conducted as a civil marriage celebrant was here on the foreshore, followed by a gala reception in the Palais. If only he had kept up his registration he could be conducting lesbian marriages on Semaphore beach today, followed by 'Palais Meltdown' receptions!

Will tells me how much he has enjoyed strolling along charming Semaphore Road by day and night for his fieldwork. Architecturally, it's a treat with many fine old buildings. It's grand to see one of Adelaide's fine 1920s movie houses, The Odeon Star, is well-maintained and still doing business. And it's locally, family-owned too! Semaphore Road brings back childhood memories for Will, the 'country bumpkin' visiting by train with his 'city-slicker cousins'. This was in the early 1960s when the trains ran right down the centre of Semaphore Road to the foreshore. Sadly, this service ceased in 1978 and the lines were uprooted. What a pity! It would be quite the tourist attraction nowadays, I'm sure. Thank goodness the tram down Jetty Road Glenelg has survived.

Semaphore has always had a strong link with neighbouring Port Adelaide as the Blue Heritage Plaque on the former Customs Boarding Station attests. You see, Semaphore was the 'outer harbour' for the Port before the real Outer Harbor opened in 1908. The beautifully restored Time Ball Tower, a towering stone structure of four storeys across the road, is another reminder of Semaphore's nautical past as the 'outer harbour' of the Port.

Let's continue our coastline cruise, shall we?

Tennyson (Estcourt) Beach

We've left our Esplanade Road and are now travelling along Military Road, the main coastal road south. On our left we have the expansive 1970s affluent suburban development of West Lakes and on our right similar modern housing, now the seaside suburb of West Lakes Shore. I believe until this suburban development, West Lakes was wild swampland, and just south of West Lake Shores were the pristine Tennyson Dunes leading to the beach and sea. Oh, look! There's the grand nineteenth-century Estcourt House, a veritable mansion of two storeys with lookout, still very prominent although now surrounded by modern housing. Wayne, a friend of Will's, recalls growing up in Largs Bay in the 1950s and, as a teenager in the mid-1960s, discovering this undeveloped swampland, sand dunes and beach. And what was his 'discovery', Rainbow History Lovers? That there was much gay fun to be had amongst the dunes and in the swamplands. This was before he had a car and he would walk all the way from Largs Bay down to Tennyson Beach. That's a seven-kilometre walk each way, Rainbow History Lovers. That is dedication! It must have been fun! Will similarly recalls having gay fun in the dunes and sea in the 1990s and 2000s which, according to his fieldwork, remains popular with gay men today.

Such was its popularity amongst beachgoers a large carpark was built off Military Road with walking paths through the dunes to the beach. Wire fencing was installed along the pathways with signage prohibiting entry to the dunes, with prosecution threatened for those who offended. I've always pondered whether this is a deliberate local government policy to deter amorous adventures amongst the dunes by beachcombers, be they gay or straight. Nowadays there are parking restrictions too. No parking 7 pm to 7 am April to September and 9 pm to 7 am October to March. In other words, no after-dark parking! As with the after-dark restriction of seaside public lavatories, I find this after-dark restriction interesting and indeed questionable. At this carpark there are gates which warn of closure in the non-parking hours. During Will's after-dark fieldwork he observed a carpark just up the road was not gated and accessible, but the gates to the large carpark leading to the well-known gay-encounter sand dunes were locked. I sense this after-dark closure of parking and dune access is a deliberate local government policy to deter gay encounters!

Rainbow History Lovers, let's continue our coastal cruise. We journey via numerous seaside suburbs, Glenelg, which you have learned so much about in the Gay Bay walk, Somerton Park, Brighton and Seacliff, all of which I'm reliably informed afforded seaside encounter opportunities! One of my informants told me of the regular fun he had with a lifesaver from the Somerton Surf Life Saving Club, for example.

Going Down in the South

Oh, Rainbow History Lovers, that term 'going down in the south' always has a particular resonance for Will. Growing up a 'sissy boy' in rural South Australia, he was teased about the way he spoke. He well recalls the time a theatrical show titled 'Down South' came to town and his excitement attending and telling his classmates of the show. One of the bully boys took exception to his pronunciation of 'down' (as in town) and brutally corrected him, 'It's down like you say brown'!

I've derailed you again, as is my wont! Let's get back on track and continue our cruise south.

From 1999 onwards the Feast program urged folk to 'go south'. In 2000, the Southern Women's Community Centre hosted a whole day of activities titled 'Going Down in the South'. Oh, Rainbow History Lovers, I'm having visuals. Was that the intention of the title, do you think? In 2001 '36 Hours in the south' was featured. The program note read:

> Adelaide's Southern region is thrilled to present a mini Feast.
> Films, forums, a cabaret and picnic.

And you know, the South just kept on giving to Feast. In 2002 there was 'Picnic By The River' – 'a day and night of extravaganza' at picturesque Market Square Park, Old Noarlunga. This park continued as the location of Southern Women's Feast Fete from 2005 to 2012. Some years it was titled Southern Women's Feast Fete and others Southern Feast Fete. It does seem to have had a strong women's focus. All members of the Rainbow community were welcome. And what an array of events were presented over these years! I adore the listing of events on offer at the first fete in 2005: musicians, women drummers, tai chi, self-defence, business owners, health information, produce growers, healers, and artists within the LGBTQIA+ communities – 'a day of fun and celebrations!' And wouldn't you know it, dog shows became an important event too. Oh, what a feast of treats, Rainbow History Lovers! I'm rather taken with women drummers and healers. What takes your fancy?

For four Feast seasons, from 2016 to 2019, Southern Pride March was added with 'fun, food, stalls and family friendly entertainment' after the march. As we all know, many festivities were interrupted by the COVID-19 pandemic. Oh, that era has been quite an interruption to our pattern of lives in many areas! Southern Pride March returned in 2021, not as part of the Feast program, but in March to coincide with Sydney's Gay and Lesbian Mardi Gras. Again in 2022 and 2023, it was held to coincide with Mardi Gras. As a committed Feaster and Adelaidean I must own to a little sadness the Southern Pride March is no longer part of Feast.

Rainbow History Lovers, 'going down in the south' would not be complete if we did not feature Maslin Beach. Again, I'm going to cheat and quote from the 1999 Feast program. Titled 'While you're here', it captures the essence of this fabulous beach:

> Maslin Beach is a kind of mecca for gay sun lovers throughout summer – it is sheltered by cliffs, covered in golden sand and washed by crystal clear waters. In 1975 Maslin Beach was declared officially as Australia's first unclad bathing area. The southern most section near the rocks has since become an unofficial gathering place for gay men (and their admirers). It gets very cruisy in summer and undercover police have been known to be on alert for beat activity.

It's both enticing and cautionary, isn't it? It's worth noting groups within the Rainbow community have different approaches to enjoying 'sun and surf'. We've heard Semaphore described as 'dyke paradise beach with great swell'. As Semaphore Helen told me, 'Women don't do the beat thing to meet each other. We were and are attracted to the seaside for recreational purposes – romantic sunsets, swimming, beach walks, walking our dogs and meeting up.' I'm sure gay men enjoy nature too, but they tend to also use the opportunity to connect in a much more physical way!

Flying the Rainbow Flag

Gertrude waving the Rainbow flag atop a municipal building.

Rainbow History Lovers, as you well know, Will and I are great believers in the importance of Rainbow visibility. Overt displays in as many ways as possible are important. Flags are so visual. The City of Adelaide has flown the Rainbow Flag from the Adelaide Town Hall during every Feast since 2011. In 2013, Feast began a campaign. It wrote to every mayor and municipal council in South Australia requesting they 'fly the flag' during Feast. Eleven participated. Over the years it has grown, with twenty-four doing so in 2022. Our stories in *Gert by Sea* are very seaside focussed. Thus, it is pleasing to observe the seaside municipalities which encompass the ground we have covered have participated in this support of our Rainbow community. The City of Port Adelaide Enfield and the City of Charles Sturt have done so since the inception of the 'Fly the Flag' campaign in 2013. The City of West Torrens joined in 2014 and the City of Holdfast Bay in 2015. Thus, all the cities along our suburban coastline now 'fly the flag' during Feast. In 2019 the City of Onkaparinga, which covers our Down South Family, joined. So, all bases are now covered, as they say. This is heart-warming indeed.

Farewell, Until the Next Walk

Gertrude inspects the carpark signage.

Farewell, Until the Next Walk

Rainbow History Lovers, this ends our *Gert by Sea* tales. It's been a delight to walk with you through two of its most distinctive suburbs, harbourside Port Adelaide and seaside Glenelg, to capture something of the character of both, and to weave Rainbow tales into both.

I also thought it important to give you a sense of the coastline, from our phallic tip of Outer Harbor down to the sun-lovers paradise of Maslin Beach. Oh, Rainbow History Lovers, 'Going Down in the South' has brought back... a distant memory. Way back, very late last century – 1999 in fact – Will was invited by the organisers of historic Willunga's very popular 'Almond Blossom Festival' to emcee at their gala picnic day and Festival Ball. It is our memory Will did the picnic day and I did the ball which climaxed with the crowning of the 'Miss Almond Blossom'. As far as we could ascertain it was a largely straight audience. They were warm and receptive. Although not the Almond Blossom Queen as such, I was a hit!

Sadly, we did not quite make it down to 'the foot' Fleurieu Peninsula. However, I understand there's quite a retiree Rainbow community right down south. I'm informed of a group of older gay denizens who've been meeting informally for coffee and meals at various venues around Goolwa and Port Elliot, and at times further afield, for close to twenty years. Birthdays are celebrated, sometimes by star signs, and the atmosphere is always welcoming and cheerful. 'What a wonderful thing for these dear older gay chaps to engage in the gift of friendship so freely, and with a minimum of fuss,' I was told.

As I mentioned Adelaide does not really have a 'Rainbow enclave'. Lesbian Semaphore may well be the closest we have. Thus, I thought it important to 'shine a light' on Semaphore in our seascape. Perhaps there is sufficient material for a complete Semaphore Rainbow History Walk... next time!

Rainbow History Lovers, my Gertrude Groupies, thank you for joining me on these two waterside walks and the coastal cruise. It really does give a new meaning to the concept of NaviGAYtion! Please remember that *Gert by Sea* is a companion to *Queen of Walk*, so always have both volumes 'on the ready'. It is only fitting that I should be celebrating all things 'seaside' in the thirtieth year of my creation and my very first history walk. It is indeed my Pearl Anniversary. I believe that I can truly claim to be 'The Pearly Queen' and '*Gert by Sea*'!

www.ingramcontent.com/pod-product-compliance
Lightning Source LLC
Chambersburg PA
CBHW041309110526
44590CB00028B/4297